HEALING HEARTBURN, NATURALLY

A Guide to Managing Acid Reflux and Restoring Gut Health

By

TIERAONA LOW DOG, MD, ABOIM

Published by:

Medicine Lodge Academy, LLC
PO Box 709
Pecos, NM 87552

DISCLAIMER—PLEASE READ CAREFULLY

Healing Heartburn, Naturally

By: Tieraona Low Dog, MD, ABOIM

ISBN: 979-8-7795-5958-4

CONTENTS

PREFACE

As a physician, I have been increasingly concerned by the ever-growing number of patients that come into the office with heartburn and leave with a prescription for a proton pump inhibitor (PPI). Many people end up taking these medications for years, and most are taking them unnecessarily.

In my own family, I witnessed my father almost die after taking a PPI for more than four years. At age 79, my father was taken by ambulance to the hospital after experiencing palpitations, severe muscle cramping and what appeared to be a small seizure. He was admitted to the hospital for a heart arrhythmia due to dangerously low magnesium levels. It took almost three days of intravenous magnesium to get his levels back into the normal range. He had been prescribed a PPI while undergoing cancer treatment, a legitimate reason to take it, but was never told to discontinue it.

A few years later, my mother at age 80 was placed on a PPI for a chronic cough that had lasted four months. She was told she had "silent" reflux, as she had no symptoms (e.g., burning, acid reflux), and that the PPI was necessary. The PPI did not improve her cough, but it was continued anyway. Almost seven months later my mother was admitted to the hospital for pneumonia, given antibiotics, and then developed *Clostridioides difficile* (*C. diff*). As you will see in this book, long-term PPI increases the risk for pneumonia, which then requires antibiotics, which increases the risk for *C. diff*, a difficult to treat and potentially life-threatening inflammation of the colon. There are even some data suggesting PPIs can increase the risk of *C. diff* directly.

These stories are all too common, especially in our elders. But I don't want to leave you with the impression that I am anti-PPI or anti-medication; that is *not* true. I do have other stories. Like the one about my friend Lou, a man who was doing construction on my home years ago. One day as I was leaving for the airport he said, "Hey Doc, can I talk to you for a minute?" He then proceeded to tell me that he had been having horrible acid reflux and chest pain for a couple of weeks that had not been relieved by over-the-counter anti-suppressive medications. He had called to get a doctor's appointment, but there wasn't one available for almost four months. I told Lou to go to the emergency room, tell them he was having severe chest pain, and they would see him promptly. I assured him they would get him taken care of much more quickly once he explained his symptoms. I returned home four days later with a message to call Lou. The long and short of it—he was diagnosed with stage four esophageal cancer and was unable to tolerate treatment—he died six weeks later. He'd been laying tile, hanging sheetrock, going up and down ladders; he seemed so strong yet, six weeks later, he was gone. Before Lou passed, he told me he'd had heartburn for as long as he could remember. He also smoked cigarettes. In Lou's case, long-term acid suppression with PPI (along with quitting tobacco) would not only have been the right thing to do, but it might also have been lifesaving.

Medications are neither good nor bad; they are just medicines. It is how they are used that determines if the risks outweigh the benefits, or vice versa. I wrote this book to help people learn how to reduce the risk of dangerous side effects if they must take long-term acid-suppression therapy. I want to help people be able to wean off PPIs safely and effectively when they are no longer indicated. Most importantly, I want to help people avoid going on these medications in the first place whenever possible.

CHAPTER 1

Heartburn and GERD — An Introduction

> *"All disease begins in the gut."*
> — HIPPOCRATES

More than 2,000 years ago, the Greek physician Hippocrates declared that "all disease begins in the gut." While that may not *entirely* be the case, science continues to show us how incredibly crucial a well-functioning gastrointestinal tract is to our overall health and wellbeing. It's not just what we eat, but how much and how quickly we eat, and our mood that impacts how well we digest and eliminate. This cycle of, eating, digesting, and eliminating of food, goes on day after day, year after year, without us paying much attention. Until, that is, something goes awry. And something often does. More than **30 million Americans** have persistent symptoms of gas, bloating, and/or constipation. Another 60 million Americans experience heartburn at least weekly, with **15 million** experiencing **heartburn daily.** Those are big numbers. While this book focuses predominantly on heartburn and gastroesophageal reflux (GERD), almost everything I recommend for putting your GI "house" in order, will help improve other minor GI problems, as well. But before we dive into recommendations, let's do a quick review of what is happening physiologically during digestion.

When food enters your mouth, the complex journey of digestion begins. As we chew food, it mixes with enzyme-rich saliva and mucus to form a mass, or bolus, that travels down our esophagus, the tube that connects our mouth to our stomach. Muscle contractions help propel food down our esophagus. There are two sphincters that keep our food moving where it is supposed to: the **upper esophageal sphincter (UES)**—which closes when we swallow to prevent the food bolus from entering our pharynx (throat)—and the **lower esophageal sphincter (LES)**, which opens when we swallow, allows the food bolus and liquids to enter our stomach, and then tightly closes to prevent the acidic contents of our stomach from reversing course. This is extremely important, as the cells that line our esophagus are very different from the cells that line our stomach. Our esophagus has *no natural defense against acid.* If the LES does not fully tighten, acid reflux can occur. When acid from the stomach backs into the esophagus, it burns the delicate esophageal lining, causing pain, burning or tightness in the chest area, behind the breastbone. This is why it is called *"heart"* burn—even though it has nothing to do with our heart. If the UES also fails, stomach acids may reach the larynx, where they can damage the vocal cords; the reflux may even reach the lungs. When the UES sphincter fails, it can cause symptoms such as chronic cough, sore throat, feeling like there is a lump in the throat, or a bitter/sour taste in the mouth. This is called **laryngopharyngeal reflux (LPR).**

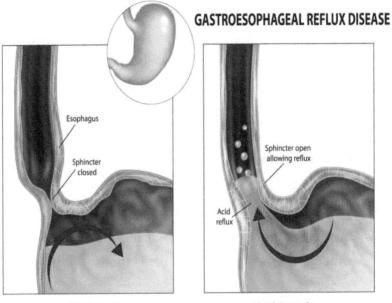

GASTROESOPHAGEAL REFLUX DISEASE

Esophagus

Sphincter closed

Sphincter open allowing reflux

Acid reflux

Healthy stomach   **Gerd stomach**

Now back to the digestion journey. As food enters our stomach it triggers G cells in the stomach to release gastrin into the bloodstream. As gastrin levels rise, HCl is released and our LES tightens. HCl (also called stomach or gastric acid) is made by the parietal cells that line the fundus and body of our stomach.

HCl is a central figure when it comes to digestion.

- **HCl destroys pathogens,** such as bacteria and yeast that enter our stomach; it is crucial for preventing gastrointestinal infections.

- HCl is necessary for **activating digestive enzymes.** Chief cells in the stomach release inactive pepsinogen, which, after exposure to HCl, converts into the powerhouse protein-digesting enzyme, **pepsin.** Activation of pepsin happens when our gastric pH is two or lower. Pepsin is **the *key* enzyme** responsible for digesting protein, reducing it to peptides for easier absorption in the small intestine. While protein digestion also occurs in our small intestine due to the action of pancreatic enzymes, our stomach is primarily where proteins are broken down. Keep this piece of information in mind later when we examine the role of stomach acid in **preventing food allergies!**

- **HCl triggers** the release of **intrinsic factor (IF),** a protein also secreted by the parietal cells. HCl and pepsin help break apart protein, releasing B12. IF then binds **vitamin B12** for transport to the farthest part of the small intestine, the ileum, where it is absorbed.

- **HCl** plays a critical role in **ionizing calcium, magnesium, potassium, iron, and zinc,** facilitating their absorption in our small intestine.

Now in order to protect our stomach from the highly corrosive effects of HCl and pepsin, **copious amounts of sticky mucus** are produced by mucus cells that cover our entire stomach cavity. This **bicarbonate-rich mucus** is 95% water and 5% of a sticky gel-like substance that allows it to adhere to and coat our stomach wall. The bicarbonate neutralizes any acid that breaches the outer protective layer of mucus.

Once our stomach has done its work, gastrin levels begin to fall, as does the production of stomach acid. The partially digested, acidic, liquified food bolus, or **chyme,** moves through our pyloric sphincter into our duodenum, the first section of our small intestine. Here, chyme stimulates the release of bicarbonate to quickly neutralize the acid, preventing damage to the duodenum. **Enzymes from our pancreas and bile from our gall bladder** flow into our small intestine to breakdown fats into fatty acids, carbohydrates into simple sugars, and peptides into amino acids for absorption into our bloodstream. In fact, our small intestine, on average about 20 feet long, is where **90% of the nutrients** in our food are absorbed. What is left, the waste, is passed along to our large intestine, which is about 5 feet long and home to the largest number of bacteria that reside in our body. These bacteria synthesize vitamin K to be absorbed and used by the body. As water and electrolytes are absorbed into our body, stool is formed and passed through our rectum and anus and then out of our body.

So, there you have it. A lightning-fast trip through the digestion of food. An elegant system, all working in harmony to extract nutrients from our food, protect us from harmful infections, and eliminate what is not needed by the body. It's a shame that stomach acid has gotten such a bad rap, given how central it is to digestion and health. And just wait until I describe what can happen if you suppress stomach acid for too long. It's shocking. Especially since acid suppression is the primary way acid reflux is managed.

Do I Have GERD?

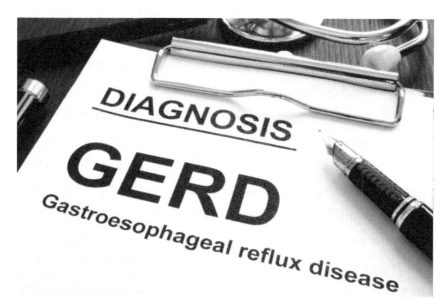

Although periodic heartburn/acid reflux can be uncomfortable, it is not generally dangerous to healthy people. Roughly **75% of people with acid reflux** have **mild symptoms** that will respond to the **lifestyle and natural therapies I recommend** in this book. But what about gastroesophageal reflux disease (GERD)? **How are heartburn and GERD different?** Well, it all comes down to the **frequency and severity** of the heartburn.

When heartburn happens *at least twice weekly*, or *moderate-to-severe reflux happens at least once per week*, it is considered GERD. Most of the time, GERD is a clinical diagnosis that your health care professional makes based upon your signs and symptoms. The **GERD-Q questionnaire** below is a quick, useful, and validated tool used to screen patients for this condition. It is considered extremely accurate for predicting GERD *if* your score is 8 or higher and you are

NOT currently taking an acid-suppressive therapy. And the best part is you can take it yourself.

Answer each question as honestly as you can. Circle the number that best fits your answer. Total all the numbers to get your GERD-Q score.

How many days per week do you experience:	Frequency Score Symptoms			
	0 day	1 day	2-3 days	4-7 days
A burning feeling behind your breastbone (heartburn)?	0	1	2	3
Stomach contents moving upwards to your throat or mouth (regurgitation)?	0	1	2	3
Pain in the center of your upper stomach area?	3	2	1	0
Nausea?	3	2	1	0
Trouble getting a good night's sleep because of heartburn or regurgitation?	0	1	2	3
Need for over-the-counter medicine for heartburn or regurgitation (such as Tums, Rolaids, Maalox) in addition to the medicine your doctor prescribed?	0	1	2	3

Scoring Results:

- Total score 0–2 points: likelihood of GERD is 0%
- Total score 3–7 points: likelihood of GERD is 50%
- Total score 8–10 points: likelihood of GERD is 79%
- Total score 11–18 points: likelihood of GERD is 89%

If you **score 8 or higher**, you should make an appointment to talk to your health care provider about your symptoms. An online version of this table can be viewed and printed by going to: https://www.aafp.org/afp/2010/0515/p1278.html - afp20100515p1278-t1 (Accessed March 10, 2021)

A Few More Important Questions

While the questionnaire is a quick way to determine if you have GERD, there are other parts of your story that should be considered when it comes to both reducing your symptoms and assessing your risk for more serious consequences from GERD.

1. **What is your age?** Yes, age does matter. If you are 65 or older and have *new symptoms* of heartburn and reflux; or if you are a white male over 50 with a multi-year history of reflux, you need to be evaluated by a GI specialist to rule out **Barrett's esophagus**, a condition in which the cells that line the esophagus become thick and inflamed after prolonged exposure to stomach acid. Barrett's esophagus is the primary precursor of esophageal adenocarcinoma—a dangerous cancer that has increased rapidly in westernized countries over the past four decades.

2. **What is your weight?** As our waistlines continue to expand, so will the prevalence of GERD. The connection between obesity and GERD is strong and multifaceted. Abdominal fat increases intra-abdominal pressure, which can push stomach contents back up into the esophagus. Abdominal fat acts like an endocrine organ, secreting hormones that cause esophageal dysmotility and relaxation of the LES, allowing

reflux to occur. Women with a body mass index (BMI) of 30 kg per m² or higher have a 2.5-fold increased risk for GERD compared to normal-weight women. Weekly heartburn and a BMI > 30 can also increase your risk for Barrett's esophagus. Of all the lifestyle interventions studied for GERD, the **strongest evidence is for weight loss**. A weight loss of 10% can significantly reduce heartburn, belching, and regurgitation. That means if you weigh 200 pounds, losing 20 pounds will dramatically improve or eliminate your symptoms. We all know how hard it is to shed those extra pounds, but even modest weight loss can help you get your heartburn under control.

3. **Use tobacco?** Smoking is strongly associated with GERD. Smoking exposes the esophagus to chemicals that damage and weaken the LES and increases the acidity in stomach fluids. If you have GERD and smoke, your odds of developing Barrett's esophagus are 51 times greater than a non-smoker. If you smoke, get the help you need to quit. Tobacco use remains the leading cause of preventable disease, disability, and death in the US. The CDC has a website with resources and information for smoking cessation programs, medications, free national and state quitlines, health coaches, and more.

4. **Do you have chronic cough or sore throat?** While the most common symptom is a burning sensation in the chest or throat, sometimes people have more silent symptoms that are easily overlooked such as sore throat, hoarseness, feeling a lump in the throat, and/or a persistent cough that lasts for more than three weeks in a non-smoker. If you have any of

these symptoms, you may be experiencing **laryngopharyngeal reflux.** Make sure you discuss your symptoms with your health care provider.

5. **How severe are your symptoms?** It's important to pay attention to the severity of your symptoms. Mild to moderate severity can often be managed with lifestyle and natural approaches; meaning you have occasional reflux that is managed by using over-the-counter antacids. More severe symptoms should be evaluated and often require a combination of lifestyle, natural approaches, and medication.

6. **How long have you had symptoms?** Long-standing GERD is harder to treat and is associated with more potential damage to the esophageal tissue. If your symptoms have persisted for months, especially in spite of treatment, you should see your primary care provider and probably a gastroenterologist (GI specialist).

7. **What is your personal and family history?** Have you ever suffered from a **bleeding ulcer?** Are you regularly **taking non-steroidal anti-inflammatory** (NSAID) medications, such as ibuprofen or aspirin? If you have a high risk for gastric bleeding, taking or staying on PPIs may be important. Have you ever been diagnosed or treated for *H. pylori,* a type of bacteria that can cause ulcers and gastric cancer? Are you sure it was completely eradicated? Have any of your first-degree relatives (e.g., mother, father, sibling) been diagnosed with **gastric cancer?** Let your health care provider know if you answered yes to any of these questions.

8. **What are your triggers?** When do you notice your symptoms? After a large meal, when bending over, after consuming alcohol, coffee, sugary foods, carbonated beverages, spicy food, tomatoes, citrus; when you are under stress, or laying down? **Keep a journal** for a few weeks. Identifying what sets off your symptoms allows you to **remove triggers**, eat smaller meals, elevate the head of your bed, etc.

9. **What have you tried?** Figure out what you've tried and assess how well it worked. Have you tried DGL (a safe form of licorice) or melatonin? Did you take or are you taking an H2 blocker or PPI? How are they working for you? If the medications are working, are you concerned about taking them long-term? If your PPI is not working, mention this to your health care provider to rule out other causes.

10. **What medications are you taking?** There are numerous medications that can cause/aggravate GERD symptoms such as statins, angiotensin-converting enzyme inhibitors (ACE-inhibitors), bisphosphonates, potassium, non-steroidal anti-inflammatories (NSAIDs), certain antibiotics (e.g., tetracycline), calcium channel blockers, benzodiazepines, quinidine, anticholinergics, tricyclic antidepressants, warfarin, beta-agonists, corticosteroids, iron, vitamin C, and others. Talk to your pharmacist to see if any of your **medications could be aggravating your GERD** and if so, talk to your health care provider for alternatives. For instance, if you take vitamin C supplements, you could switch to a buffered product. For a list of medications that can aggravate GERD, click here.

11. **Are you pregnant?** GERD is relatively common during the second and third trimesters. This is because the hormone progesterone, which is high in pregnancy, reduces lower esophageal sphincter tone making reflux more likely. **Lifestyle recommendations and calcium/magnesium-based antacids are generally effective.** Talk to your midwife or physician about what is right for you.

Stop: Do You Have Any "Red Flags?"

Before we go any further, let's make sure you don't have any "red flags" that could indicate something more serious going on with your reflux. These include:

- **Unintended weight loss**
- **Bloody stools**
- Frequent **vomiting or vomiting blood**

- **Difficult or painful swallowing**, particularly of solid foods
- Iron deficiency anemia
- Chest pain
- 65 years or older with new onset of reflux symptoms
- White male 50 years or older with multi-year reflux symptoms
- Obese (BMI> 30 kg per m2) with persistent reflux symptoms
- Smoke tobacco and have persistent reflux symptoms
- Have persistent reflux in spite of taking adequate acid suppression therapy

If you answered yes to any of the above, *you need to see your physician and/or a GI specialist for further evaluation*. If you are taking any acid-suppressive medications, *under* no circumstances should you discontinue them without talking to your health care provider first.

CHAPTER 2

Conventional Treatments for Heartburn and GERD

The most common approach for treating acid reflux is to either neutralize the acid or shut it down altogether. No acid, no reflux! Without HCl, pepsin cannot be activated, and pepsin is a major problem when it comes to damaging esophageal tissue. While suppressing HCl is highly effective, it might surprise you to know that **GERD is almost never the result of *excessive* stomach acid**, except in rare conditions such as Zollinger-Ellison syndrome. The problem for most people with GERD is **transient relaxation of the LES,** which allows acidic stomach contents (and sometimes duodenal contents) to move up into the esophagus.

Acid Suppression Therapies

While hypersecretion of stomach acid is not the primary problem, **acid-suppressive therapies** are the primary treatment for GERD because few drugs adequately address gastric dysmotility and impaired LES function. (In Chapter 5, I discuss the role of **melatonin** for this). There are three primary types of pharmaceuticals used for the management of GERD: **antacids, H-2 receptor antagonists (H-2 blockers), and PPIs.**

Antacids

Antacids are substances/products that **neutralize acids** in the stomach. They generally contain calcium, magnesium, or aluminum with carbonate, hydroxide, or sodium bicarbonate. These act as weak bases to counteract acid, making the gastric pH more neutral. Alkaline water, for which there is a small amount of research, may also fit into the antacid category. Antacids are considered very safe for occasional use with just a few caveats:

- Products containing **sodium** should be avoided or used judiciously if you have high blood pressure or poor kidney function.
- **Calcium based antacids** can interfere with the absorption of iron, bisphosphonates and tetracycline and should be taken at least four hours apart.
- **Aluminum antacids** can cause constipation and contribute to weakening of the bones. Taken in excess over prolonged periods, they could lead to aluminum toxicity.

- **Magnesium antacids** may cause diarrhea in some individuals. However, since many Americans don't get enough magnesium in their diet, this **might be a good choice.**

H2 Blockers

H2 blockers **block histamine receptors.** Histamine is one of three triggers for stomach acid production, the other two are acetylcholine and gastrin. H2 blockers were the mainstay of GERD treatment until PPIs were introduced into the market. PPIs block all three triggers, giving a more complete and potent inhibition of gastric acid.

H2 blockers can be effective for those with **mild-to-moderate forms of GERD** and are often used as part of a step-down approach when **tapering off PPIs.** Common H2 blockers include famotidine (Pepcid™), cimetidine (Tagamet™), and nizatidine (Axid™). **Taken before the first and last meal of the day, and/or at bedtime,** most people experience relief within one hour and that relief can last several hours. Headache is the most commonly reported adverse effect. Those with kidney disorders should not take famotidine.

Note: The popular H2 blocker **ranitidine** (Zantac™) was found to contain low levels of N-nitrosodimethylamine (NDMA), a potential carcinogen, and in April 2020, the FDA issued a notice to discontinue sale of prescription and over the counter versions of this drug.

Proton Pump Inhibitors (PPIs)

PPIs were introduced in 1989 and literally transformed our ability to effectively treat acid-related disorders. These drugs **inhibit the final common pathway** of stomach acid production, regardless of the mechanism of stimulation (histamine, gastrin, or acetylcholine). They maintain a **gastric pH >5** for 15 to 21 hours per day, far longer than H2 blockers. More than 113 million PPI prescriptions are written each year, with sales topping $13 billion in 2015. With the availability of over-the-counter PPIs, the number of actual users is much larger than these numbers suggest. The high rate of PPI use is not just a US phenomenon; their use is increasing globally.

The Food and Drug Administration (FDA) has approved this class of medications for the following indications in adults:

- Healing of **erosive esophagitis**
- **Maintenance** of healed erosive esophagitis
- Treatment of gastroesophageal reflux disease (GERD)
- Risk reduction for **gastric ulcer** associated with nonsteroidal anti-inflammatory drugs
- *H. pylori* **eradication** to reduce the risk of duodenal ulcer, in combination with antibiotics
- **Pathological hypersecretory conditions,** including Zollinger-Ellison syndrome
- Short-term treatment and maintenance of **duodenal ulcers**

Not every PPI is approved for each of these conditions. A full list of PPI medications, their indication, dose and recommended duration can be found here for adults and here for children. It is absolutely appropriate to use these medications long-term in some patients (e.g., Zollinger-Ellison syndrome, maintenance of erosive esophagitis, high risk of GI bleeding, etc.), however, **2–8 weeks of treatment** is what is recommended for treating frequent heartburn,

GERD, the healing of ulcers, and as part of a protocol for eradicating *H. pylori*.

Unfortunately, PPIs are often taken far longer than necessary. Reports of inappropriate PPI prescribing and use are widespread, ranging from **40–63%** in medical literature. And because acid-suppressive therapies are also available over the counter, many people take them for long periods without any monitoring. If these drugs were completely benign, that would be one thing, but they are not. **Long-term acid suppression can lead to numerous health problems, some of them very serious.**

CHAPTER 3

The Downside of Acid Suppression

There are people who greatly benefit from taking medications to suppress stomach acid, however, many people have been prescribed PPI medications inappropriately and/or take them far longer than recommended by FDA guidelines. What's more: 75% of people with acid reflux have minor symptoms that are *completely amenable* to lifestyle and natural approaches. This is important to know, as these medications can be difficult to wean off and their long-term use is associated with numerous adverse effects.

Rebound Acid Hypersecretion

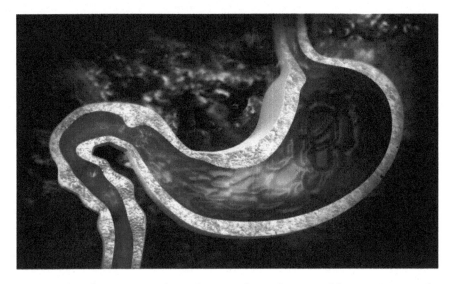

People often stay on PPIs longer than they need because it can be hard to stop taking them. When food enters our stomach, G cells produce gastrin, which is released into our bloodstream. As serum gastrin levels rise, the parietal cells in our stomach begin to secrete stomach acid, and our LES tightens. As acid is pumped into our stomach cavity, pH levels fall, and so does serum gastrin. Any medication that significantly shuts down stomach acid will cause gastrin levels to remain elevated, as the normal feedback loop is impaired. So, **when one suddenly stops taking their PPI, the elevated gastrin in their bloodstream causes a surge in acid production.**

Many clinicians (myself included) have seen this problem in practice, but it was also clearly demonstrated in a clinical trial. A double-blind placebo-controlled study randomized 120 healthy individuals *without reflux* to twelve weeks of placebo or eight weeks of esomeprazole (Nexium™, 40 mg per day) followed by four weeks of placebo. At the end of the trial, **44% of those in the PPI group had at least one acid-related symptom** during weeks 9–12 (when switched to placebo) compared to only 15% in the placebo group. The number of people reporting dyspepsia, heartburn, or acid regurgitation in the PPI group was 22% at weeks 10 and 11 and 21% at week 12. Corresponding figures in the placebo group were 7%, 5%, and 2% at weeks 10, 11, and 12, respectively.

While some people can stop taking PPIs "cold turkey," many require a tapered approach to reduce the risk of rebound acid production. Patients have repeatedly told me, "Doc, I tried going off my heartburn medication, but when I stopped, my heartburn was worse than it was before I started taking them." To address this issue, I have written an entire protocol for weaning off PPI medications in Chapter 11.

The Gut Microbiome and Infection

Stomach acid plays a crucial role in maintaining a healthy gut microbiome, which is comprised of billions of microorganisms (microbiota)—including bacteria, fungi, viruses, and parasites. The largest concentrations of microbiota are in our small and large intestines, where, in healthy individuals, there is a balance between beneficial and potentially harmful microbes. Maintaining this balance is crucial for our nutritional, immunological, and metabolic wellbeing.

Stomach acid directly destroys harmful pathogens as they enter our stomach, which is essential for preventing GI infections. When acid is shut down by PPIs, up to 50% of salivary and ingested bacteria survive by slipping past this ingenious "gastric acid trap." These translocated bacteria disrupt the normal gut microbiota, leading to a condition called dysbiosis. When dysbiosis occurs in the small intestine, it is called **small intestinal bacterial overgrowth, or SIBO.** PPIs clearly increase the risk for SIBO. While many people do not notice any symptoms, some experience pain after meals, indigestion, gas, bloating, diarrhea, and/or constipation. In severe cases, malnutrition and weight loss can occur.

With 70% of our immune system located within and around our GI tract: it is a critical line of defense. By altering the balance between beneficial and pathogenic microbes, PPIs can increase the risk for GI infections. Dangerous infections. In February 2012, the FDA issued safety warnings stating that PPI medications can increase the risk for *Clostridioides difficile* infection (CDI; formerly *Clostridium difficile*). *C. difficile* is a bacterium that can cause life-threatening diarrhea and inflammation of the colon. This infection is most often associated with taking antibiotics as you are 7–10 times more likely to get CDI during or within one month after taking an antibiotic. PPIs, however, can also cause CDI. After reviewing 56 studies that included over

356,000 people, reviewers found one has double the odds of getting CDI if taking a PPI compared to a non-user. PPI users also have an increased risk for developing other diarrhea-causing intestinal infections, including *Salmonella* and *Campylobacter*. Evidence shows that people taking PPIs have roughly *five times the odds* of developing these GI infections when compared to non-users. The FDA website states you "should seek immediate care if you are taking a PPI and develop diarrhea that does not improve." Wow.

Although the relationship is less consistent, some studies also show that long-term PPI use can increase the risk for community-acquired **pneumonia** (this means you didn't get the infection in a hospital or nursing home). Without adequate stomach acid production, there can be an overgrowth of oropharyngeal bacteria, which increases the risk for infection. A review of 26 studies found a 1.5-fold increase in risk for community-acquired pneumonia, with the highest risk occurring within 30 days of starting PPIs. This may be particularly dangerous for elders, who are already at a higher risk of developing and dying from pneumonia.

We are still learning about SARS-CoV-2 (COVID-19). However, we know the virus can enter our body through the GI system, bind to the widely expressed angiotensin-converting enzyme-2 (ACE-2) receptor, and replicate rapidly within the cells that line our intestine. Both live infectious virus and viral RNA were in the stools of up to 50% of people with COVID-19 even when the virus was not present in the respiratory tract. The GI tract appears to be a significant portal of entry. One study found those taking PPIs have a higher risk of testing positive for COVID-19, especially when taking these medications twice per day. A large study from Korea found that among those with confirmed COVID-19, the current use of PPIs conferred a 79% greater risk of **severe clinical outcomes,** and that risk climbed to 90% if PPI use started within 30 days of the infection. This research is consistent with a US-based study that found that **mortality** from COVID-19 **was 2.3 times higher in PPI users** compared to non-users.

This increased risk for infection is not limited to adults. A review of 14 studies found a significant association between acid-suppressive therapies and the risk of **gastrointestinal infections, sepsis, and pneumonia in infants**. Roughly 70–85 % of infants experience regurgitation/reflux within the first two months of life, which resolves on its own in 95 % of babies by their first birthday. PPIs are prescribed frequently for this problem—even though both national and international pediatric GI guidelines strongly recommend against using acid suppression therapy for infant gastroesophageal reflux.

Food Allergies

The secretion of stomach acid triggers the activation of pepsin, the key enzyme involved in the breakdown of proteins. If you shut down stomach acid, you shut down pepsin. This may increase the risk for— or worsening of—food allergies, as it is the *proteins* in a specific food that your immune system reacts to when if you are **allergic** to a particular food. Food allergies are on the rise; it is estimated the rate has more than doubled since 1960. Once thought to be a condition that primarily impacted children, we now know that adults can—*and do*—develop new food allergies. Up to 10% of American adults have a food allergy. Food allergies can dramatically impact an individual's quality of life and can be life-threatening if severe.

So, what happens when one is allergic to a particular food? When the immune system overreacts to what would typically be an innocuous substance—such as soy or peanuts—the body produces a particular type of antibody called **IgE**. Upon repeat exposure to the food, these antibodies travel to cells that release chemicals causing classic allergic symptoms (e.g., nasal congestion, throat tightness, lip swelling, hives, etc.). One of the methods for identifying suspected food allergies is testing for specific IgE antibodies in the blood. A high IgE level generally confirms the diagnosis.

Though the increase of people with food allergies is undeniably a multifactorial and complex issue, PPIs may be playing a role. In 2005, a study of 152 adults treated for three months with acid-suppressive therapy (H2 blockers or PPIs) found an *increase* in IgE antibody formation in 10% of patients, and *new* IgE formation in 15% of patients compared to baseline. This means that some people with food allergies experienced **heightened sensitivity,** and **15% developed completely new food allergies** within **just 12 weeks of starting acid-suppressive therapy**.

This same phenomenon has been reported in children. Reviewers found that a history of acid-suppressive therapy was associated with an **increased prevalence of food allergies in children,** while another study found that children with GERD taking acid suppressive medications were **3.67 times more likely to be diagnosed with a food allergy** compared to a well-matched control group. Some research suggests that acid suppression may even aggravate or worsen reactions in those with **seasonal allergies.**

Vitamin B12 Deficiency

Stomach acid is necessary for triggering the release of intrinsic factor (IF) from the stomach parietal cells. The job of IF is to bind with **vitamin B12** and transport it to our small intestine for absorption. Vitamin B12 is essential for the maintenance of blood and nerve cells, the formation of cellular DNA, and plays a key role in maintaining physical energy and mental health. **As we age,** we naturally produce **less stomach acid,** which impairs our ability to absorb food-bound vitamin B12. For this reason, the Food and Nutrition Board recommends that people 50 years and older, eat foods *fortified* with B12 and/or take a vitamin B12 *supplement* because supplemental B12 does not require stomach acid or IF.

Given what we know about stomach acid and vitamin B12, it shouldn't come as a surprise that there are concerns about B12 deficiency developing in those taking PPIs long-term. While many people have a couple years of vitamin B12 stored in their liver, a 2015 meta-analysis of studies found an 80% increased risk of B12 deficiency after just *ten months* of daily PPI use. And it isn't just the lack of stomach acid that can cause vitamin B12 levels to fall. **In SIBO,** the increased numbers of bacteria in the small intestine use B12 for fuel, causing levels to decline. Many people with type-2 diabetes take **metformin,** which definitely lowers serum B12, and these patients often take it alongside a PPI. A double whammy when it comes to vitamin B12.

Some symptoms of vitamin B12 deficiency, such as loss of appetite, loss of taste and smell, difficulty walking, tingling/numbness in hands and feet, joint pain, memory problems and even dementia, are often overlooked and written off as "just a part of aging." Unfortunately, long-term B12 deficiency can cause irreversible nerve damage. If you are taking metformin and/or a PPI long-term (longer than one year), it is worthwhile having your vitamin B12 levels checked annually.

Magnesium Deficiency

Stomach acid is necessary for the ionization and absorption of certain minerals. Magnesium is the fourth most abundant mineral in the human body and plays a pivotal role in providing energy for metabolic processes, nourishing the nervous system, assisting in muscle contraction and relaxation, and maintaining cardiovascular health. Government surveys show that around half of Americans do not meet the recommended daily intake from diet alone. And we know that certain drugs can also deplete the body of magnesium over time.

In March 2011, the FDA warned that long-term PPI use (generally longer than one year) can cause **dangerously low magnesium levels, or hypomagnesemia.** A 2015 meta-analysis of nine observational studies with a total of 109,798 patients found a 63% increased risk of hypomagnesemia in those taking PPIs, compared to non-users. And a 2018 review of patients hospitalized for extreme hypomagnesemia found that 70% were taking PPIs.

Alarmingly, in roughly 25 percent of people who develop PPI-induced hypomagnesemia, magnesium supplementation does not correct the deficiency—the medication must be stopped. When these patients restarted their PPI, magnesium levels plummeted again. Low magnesium levels are associated with elevated blood pressure, heart arrhythmias, insulin resistance, type-2 diabetes, migraine headaches, and metabolic syndrome. The FDA recommends that health care providers "Consider obtaining serum magnesium levels prior to initiation of prescription PPI treatment and **checking levels periodically** thereafter for patients expected to be on prolonged treatment or who take PPIs with medications such as digoxin or drugs that may cause hypomagnesemia (e.g., diuretics). Advise patients to **seek immediate care** from a healthcare professional if they experience arrhythmias, tetany [muscle spasms], tremors, or seizures while taking PPIs. These **may be signs of hypomagnesemia.**"

This FDA recommendation, which seems so sensible and proactive, is in contrast with guidance from the American Gastroenterology Association that instructs clinicians *not* to routinely screen or monitor magnesium in patients taking long-term PPIs. Given the devastating consequences of low magnesium, why not screen, particularly in those who are diabetic, elder, or taking other drugs that might increase the risk of hypomagnesemia? My father almost died from an arrhythmia due to PPI-induced hypomagnesemia.

Increased Risk of Fracture

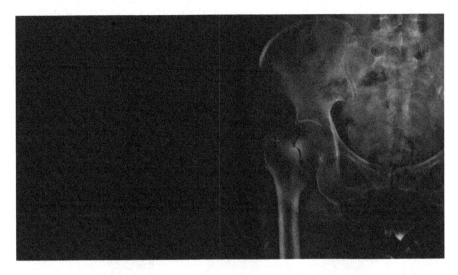

Calcium absorption, like magnesium, is also impaired with long-term PPI use. When calcium levels fall, parathyroid hormone is triggered, which moves calcium out of the bone to maintain adequate calcium levels in the blood. Over time, this can deteriorate the bone, increasing the risk for fracture. In 2010, the FDA mandated a warning on PPI labels of an increased risk of osteoporosis-related fractures.

Fragility fractures are associated with decreased quality of life, increased disability, more frequent hospital admissions and an increased risk of mortality. Approximately 75% of hip, spine and forearm fractures occur in those 65 years or older. Based on the available literature, there appears to be a **25–50% increased risk in hip fracture** associated with the use of PPIs, though not all studies show this same risk and there appears to be variation based upon the specific PPI studied. Regardless, overmedication of elders is common, and many wind-up taking PPIs for years. Many of the patients I've seen, 70 years of age and older, have not been evaluated for their calcium intake, had their vitamin D level checked, or been recommended physical or occupational therapy for fall reduction.

Cognitive Impairment

Given that PPIs are often prescribed to older adults, it is concerning that there are reports suggesting long-term PPI use can impair cognition. Animal models show that PPIs cross the blood-brain barrier where they can inhibit proton pumps in the membranes of microglial cells that are responsible for clearing away pathogens and beta-amyloid in the brain. Beta-amyloid can form plaques, which **contributes to the development of Alzheimer's dementia.**

When evaluating a German cohort of 73,679 participants 75 years of age or older, and free of dementia at baseline, researchers found a 44% increased risk of dementia in those taking PPIs, compared to non-users. While a systemic review found a positive association in the majority of 11 studies exploring cognitive impairment, the researchers found it difficult to reach any definitive conclusion about the relationship of PPIs and dementia given the problems with methodology and conflicting results. Dementia is a slow progressive multifactorial process and at this time, it is simply not possible to know what role, if any, long-term PPI use may play. But it is something to consider if you have a strong family history of dementia or are living with a loved one who is struggling with cognitive decline.

Whether or not PPIs influence the progression of dementia, the impact on cognition may be very real. A 2015 study randomized 60 young healthy volunteers to one of five different PPI drugs or a placebo for one week. Participants were administered the Cambridge Neuropsychological Test Automated Battery (CANTAB), once at baseline and again at the conclusion of the one-week study, to assess cognitive impairment. Even with this short-term use in healthy young people, it was evident that *all PPIs* have some **"exacerbated effects on cognition,"** though esomeprazole showed less impact on cognitive function than others.

The American Geriatrics Society **recommends *against* the use of PPIs** for longer than eight weeks in older adults, except in high-risk patients. If you are taking a PPI long-term and it seems like it is affecting your memory, thinking or mood, make sure you talk to your health care provider.

Kidney Damage

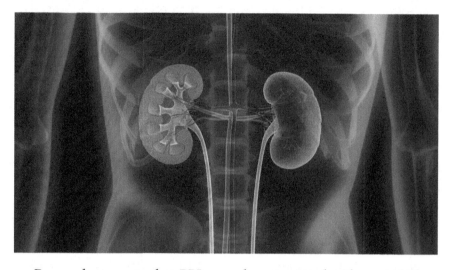

Research suggests that PPIs may be *associated* with acute kidney injury, acute interstitial nephritis (a swelling of the kidney tubules), chronic kidney disease, kidney disease progression, kidney failure, and an increased risk of dying from chronic kidney disease. It was initially thought that PPIs were mostly associated with acute kidney injury, however, there is a growing body of evidence that they can also lead to chronic kidney disease.

The Atherosclerosis Risk in Communities study followed 10,439 people without kidney disease at baseline for almost 14 years and found the risk of chronic kidney disease was 50% greater in people taking PPIs compared to non-users. The number needed to harm was 30, meaning that for every 30 people that took PPIs, one experienced kidney injury. Using the Veterans Affairs National Database, researchers found a similar risk of chronic kidney disease, the risk increasing with duration of use. And in 2018, when researchers examined five studies that included a total of 662,624 people, they also found that chronic PPI use was associated with a deterioration in kidney function. The longer someone took the medication, the greater the risk for progression to end-stage renal disease (ESRD).

From an editorial in the *Journal of the American Society of Nephrology*, "In the end, the message for physicians and patients is that PPI use should be discouraged when a clear-cut indication does not exist, despite the apparent short-term safety. In those who require PPI therapy to treat acid-related gastrointestinal disease, some form of surveillance (serum creatinine and/or urinalysis testing) should probably be undertaken."

Gastric Cancer

Stomach, or gastric cancer, is the fifth most common cancer, and the third leading cause of cancer-related death, globally. Risk factors for gastric cancer include *H. pylori* infection, smoking, alcohol, obesity, and possibly the frequent consumption of cured red meats.

H. pylori is a chronic infection has been classified by the World Health Organization as a carcinogen since 1994, and is responsible for roughly 78% of all gastric cancers.

Treatment for H. *pylori* consists of multiple antibiotics, bismuth-containing medication, and a PPI-necessary to elevate the gastric pH (make the stomach less acidic) so the antibiotics can kill the bacteria. However, there is growing bacterial resistance to commonly used antibiotics, and failure to eradicate H. *pylori*. Some experts believe the link between PPIs and gastric cancer is primarily due to failure to eliminate H. *pylori* infection. Though researchers have found that even after successful eradication, long-term PPI use is still associated with double the risk of gastric cancer.

A large population-based study from Sweden that evaluated virtually every adult (797,067 people) placed on maintenance therapy with PPIs from 2005–2012, found a three-fold increased risk for esophageal and gastric cancer. In 2019, a systematic review of seven studies that included more than 943,070 patients concluded that those who used PPIs for more than 36 months were more likely to develop gastric cancer. This was true even in those who had H. *pylori* eradicated.

With chronic acid suppression comes an overgrowth of bacteria species in the stomach that drive inflammation. Then there is the role of the hormone gastrin. Gastrin—a major stimulator of gastric acid secretion—is released from G cells in the stomach where it binds to the CCK-B (cholecystokinin-B) receptor. Unfortunately, it turns out that CCK-B receptors are often overexpressed in gastric cancers and result is tumor proliferation when activated by gastrin. In other words, gastrin can have a pro-growth effect on gastric cancer. PPIs shut down stomach acid production, causing gastrin levels to remain elevated, as there is nothing to dial it back.

The linkage between long-term use of PPIs and gastric cancer is by no means settled science. As I've said many times, there is a rational reason for some people to take PPIs for long periods of time. However, given all the information that I have just presented, it should also be crystal clear that it is just as important to not keep anyone on them longer than what is medically necessary.

CHAPTER 4
Diet and Acid Reflux

> *"Let thy food be thy medicine, and thy medicine*
> *be thy food."*
> — HIPPOCRATES

Or, as I like to say: **"If you truly want to change the trajectory of your health, start with what, when, and how you eat."** In both my professional and personal life, I have found that how we nourish ourselves affects us on many levels. Decades ago, while traveling through Italy and France, I fell in love with the food and the rituals surrounding it—the flavors and freshness, the smaller portion sizes, the slow pace of the meals, and the calming walks after dinner. When I returned home, I bought more cut flowers, spent a little more money on better olive oil and balsamic vinegar, and used more fresh herbs in my cooking. While I did not adopt the late dinner time (often 8 PM or later), our evening meal continues to be a slow and relaxed affair.

Every evening after dinner, we take the dogs for a 30-minute walk, which is good for them and us. Our food is organic and/or locally grown, rich in plants, and minimally processed. Water is my primary beverage of hydration, with tea in the morning and a glass of wine in the evening. We practice intermittent fasting, eating between 11 AM and 7 PM. At my last primary care appointment, my physical exam and labs came back glowing. I had no sign of insulin resistance, cholesterol problems, inflammation, hypertension, nutrient deficiencies, or anything else one might expect to find in a woman in her 60s. Eating healthy is not hard. It is wonderful and enjoyable. And most importantly—it is the foundation for a healthy life.

Our digestion and reflux are influenced by **what, when, how much, and how quickly** we eat and drink—as well as our **emotional** state. The recommendations made in this section, while specific for heartburn, are foundational for anyone.

- *Eat early and take an evening walk.* The advice not to eat *within 3 hours* of laying down is solid. Late-night dinners are not your friend if you struggle with heartburn, as they will increase gastric acid production not long before bed. After dinner, take a walk. In addition to the many health benefits of movement, the old tradition of taking an evening stroll stimulates gastric emptying, moving food through the stomach and small intestine more quickly, helping prevent reflux. Make it a habit. You'll find that not only do you have less reflux and bloating, but you'll sleep better, too.

- *Eat less.* Large meals distend your stomach, pushing its contents back up into your esophagus. And stop snacking. Every time you eat or have a soft drink between meals, you *secrete gastric acid.* This may contribute to loss of LES tone over time.

- *Eat slowly.* When you eat quickly, you swallow more air, causing gas, bloating, and yes, heartburn. I still remember my mother telling me to chew my food 30 times before swallowing. It was so annoying. But she was right. Chewing your food more thoroughly, means less work and less time in your stomach.

- *Relax when you eat.* Since hormones and nerves regulate our LES, stress can alter its function. The gut-brain connection is real. Sitting down to eat while fuming about work, being worried about the kids, or anxious over tomorrow can all disrupt digestion and aggravate GI problems. When our daughter was a younger, my husband and I would take turns reading from *A Grateful Heart* before dinner. It helped us quiet and settle, setting the stage for a relaxing dinner. Mindful eating habits can be very beneficial not only for GERD but also for managing weight and changing your relationship with food.

- *Journal to identify triggers.* Keep a journal to track what you eat and drink and your symptoms. The most frequently reported food triggers are peppermint, chocolate, garlic, onions, citrus, tomato products, fried foods, spicy foods, coffee, alcohol and carbonated beverages. Peppermint, chocolate, coffee, and alcohol relax our LES. Spicy and acidic foods (and beverages) can directly irritate our esophageal tissue. Carbonated liquids cause distension of our stomach and transient lowering of LES pressure. Fried foods take longer to digest, meaning the acidic contents of your stomach sit around longer. While these foods are frequently referred to as the big "no-nos" for GERD, studies are conflicting; and what may bother one person doesn't seem to bother another. This is why journaling to identify *your* triggers is so important.

The Relationship Between Fat, Protein, Carbohydrate, and Acid Reflux

When it comes to the relationship between GERD and the macronutrients—fat, protein, and carbohydrates—the evidence is evolving and doesn't follow a straight line. For decades, clinicians have been telling people with reflux to follow a "low fat" diet. This makes sense as we know that fat can decrease LES pressure and delay gastric emptying, which can cause reflux; and people often identify fried foods as a trigger for their reflux. But studies that actually measure pH and reflux, *in addition to* participant diaries, have found that is **high calorie** meals, *independent* of fat content, that are most *strongly associated with acid reflux.* High caloric meals increase distension and cause relaxation of the LES. Interestingly though, in these studies, participants *experience* more discomfort (e.g., gas and bloating) with higher fat meals, which may explain why people with GERD complain of symptoms even though pH studies do not consistently show any increase in esophageal acid exposure.

There also may be a difference between men and women when it comes to fat and reflux. Research suggests that higher fat intake, regardless of type; is positively associated with reflux symptoms *in men,* but *not in women.* This difference, if real, is not understood. Though almost every expert group recommends going on a low-fat diet for reflux, when taken in totality, the research does not support a *consistent* link between dietary fat and reflux. Having said that, from an overall health perspective, I recommend you dramatically reduce fried/greasy foods in your diet, and opt instead for baked/grilled veggies, seafood, poultry and lean red meats.

If fat is not the biggest problem, what about carbohydrates? The evidence is actually stronger for the relationship between dietary sugar, high glycemic load diets and heartburn. The glycemic load is a measure of how much and how quickly a standard serving size of food causes your blood sugar and insulin levels to rise. Highly refined grains and sugary foods/beverages have a high glycemic load, as do French fries and white rice. Let's look at some of the main tenets of a low glycemic load diet:

- Eat more "non-starchy" carbs (e.g., berries, apples, veggies, zucchini, green peas, lentils)
- Eat more minimally processed whole grains (e.g., brown rice, steel cut oats, stone-ground bread)
- Eat some protein and fat with every meal
- Limit "white" foods (e.g., white potatoes, white rice, white bread)
- Limit concentrated sweets (e.g., sugar sweetened beverages, ice cream, donuts, cookies)

A low glycemic load diet is a solid recommendation for everyone. The research shows that this way of eating can reduce the risk of obesity, insulin resistance, type-2 diabetes, heart disease, and certain cancers, including gastric cancer. A low glycemic load diet is considered to be < 80 while a high glycemic load is considered to be > 120 (to learn more look at the Resources at the end of this chapter).

When it comes to carbohydrates and reflux, it is the starch and disaccharides (e.g., sucrose, lactose) that appear to be the most problematic, as they are only partially absorbed in the small intestine. When consumed in large amounts, as is common in the diet of many Americans, they undergo fermentation in the large intestine, releasing hormones that cause relaxation of the LES. A cross-sectional study of 2,987 adults found that high glycemic load diets were associated with a *significantly increased risk of reported heartburn* and/or chronic dyspepsia/indigestion. When you cut back on sugars and starch, such as in a low glycemic load diet, it can reduce reflux, as you will see below.

A 2018 Italian study of 130 people with gastritis and/or gastritis with reflux rotated through three two-week treatment arms: (1) Mediterranean diet plus acidic foods (juice of two lemons and ~ 100 g fresh orange tomato without seeds eaten raw or cooked/peeled); (2) very low glycemic load diet (mostly protein and fat), and (3) very low glycemic load diet (mostly protein and fat) plus the acidic foods previously mentioned. There was a 2 week wash out between each treatment arm. A dramatic improvement in symptoms was seen in the very low glycemic load treatment arms with or without acidic foods. Interesting researchers included citrus and tomatoes as they are acidic foods, which are often associated with reflux. They hypothesized that the acidic foods would help lower gastric pH, shutting down further production of HCl and eliminating or reducing GERD. Many people use apple cider vinegar (pH 2) in a similar way, drinking a small shot with a meal to aid digestion.

In a study of 144 obese women, heartburn symptoms were assessed at baseline and again after consuming a high-fat/low-carbohydrate diet for 16 weeks in 44 women with *both* obesity and GERD. Many were taking prescription meds *plus* over-the-counter meds for breakthrough reflux. At baseline, the *glycemic load* was high at 193.6 ± 51.4 for those with GERD *versus* 166.5 ± 60.0 in women without GERD. Wow! High glycemic loads in both groups! However, after dramatically eliminating starchy carbs and added sugars, the glycemic load dropped all the way down to 72–82 per day by the end of the study. By the end of week 10, *all GERD symptoms* and *medication* usage had resolved in *all* women. Fat was higher, carbs were dramatically lower, and GERD resolved. Interesting....

What happens if we objectively measure the impact of carbohydrates on reflux? Researchers did just that in a study of 12 people with GERD. After taking patients off their acid blocking medications for one week and having them each undergo an endoscopic exam, participants were given a 500 ml liquid meal containing either 84.8 grams or 178.9 grams of carbohydrates (protein and fat content same in both). Each person consumed both liquid meals while undergoing pH monitoring. Participants had significantly more reflux periods of longer duration after the high carbohydrate meal, compared to the lower carbohydrate meal.

What about protein? There has been less focus placed on this micronutrient. A questionnaire given to patients with GERD found protein consumption in the evening was inversely associated with GERD symptoms. As expected, the survey also noted that people who ate a large meal in the evening had more GERD symptoms, as was eating dinner within 2 hours of bedtime.

The type of protein might matter. A pilot study of 165 patients with heartburn found that vegetable protein caused less reflux in the one hour following the meal, than animal protein. While the evidence linking red meat, and particularly processed red meat (e.g., ham, bacon, hot dogs, sausages), to gastric cancer is mixed, it is still wise to limit processed meat in your diet, especially if you are already at higher risk (e.g., family history of gastric cancer, long-term use of PPIs, obese, smoker). Substituting some animal protein for vegetable protein is a healthy idea all around.

What do I recommend? A **low glycemic load, Mediterranean leaning diet** within an 8-hour window. A **keto**-leaning diet may also be a useful approach, particularly if you are trying to lose weight, however, it can be hard to stick with. As with most things, you have to find what works best for you. If you want to change your health, a good place to start is with what and how you eat.

CHAPTER 5

Sleep, Melatonin, and Reflux

Ensuring a good night's sleep is important for everyone. Our body repairs itself, and our brain consolidates memories while we sleep. We have all felt the consequences of a bad night's sleep but persistent sleep problems increase your risk for depression, pain, heart disease, diabetes, and traffic accidents. If you're struggling with getting enough ZZ's, you're not alone: 70 million Americans have problems falling or staying asleep. And we know that there is a **bidirectional relationship between reflux and sleep**. Treating nighttime reflux improves sleep and improving sleep quality can reduce reflux. A smaller dinner eaten earlier in the evening will go a long way to reducing nighttime troubles. As mentioned earlier, do NOT lay down within 3 hours after eating. Sleep position also matters. Sleeping on your back or stomach can lead to the flow of stomach contents back into your esophagus and throat. Sleeping on your right side is also bad if you have reflux, as the acid pocket in your upper stomach is closer to your esophageal stomach junction. *Sleeping on your **left side** is the very best position!* Elevating the head of your bed with blocks (10–12 inches) or sleeping on a wedge pillow can also bring some relief.

But what if I told you that a certain hormone could impact both your reflux and your insomnia? If you guessed melatonin, you're right! The melatonin secreted by our pineal gland is crucially important for maintaining our sleep-wake cycle. It is suppressed during exposure to blue light (sunlight) and released with increasing darkness. There is strong and compelling evidence that melatonin supplementation is highly effective for shortening the time it takes to fall asleep by resetting our biological clock. It works especially well for those whose sleep is delayed two or more hours beyond their 'normal' bedtime (delayed sleep phase disorder). For both of these purposes, melatonin is taken 1.5–2 hours *before* the desired bedtime. If you **want to fall asleep at 10 PM, take your melatonin at 8 PM**. Most people mistakenly take it when they go to bed, thinking it works like a sleeping pill. It doesn't.

Interestingly, a special group of cells in our GI tract—the enteroendocrine cells—make more than 400 times the melatonin than what is produced by our pineal gland. The amount of melatonin in our GI tract is 10–100 times greater than what is in our bloodstream. And unlike the melatonin in our pineal gland, which responds to light and darkness, the release of melatonin in our GI tract is dramatically increased by food intake, particularly tryptophan-rich protein. (Tryptophan is a precursor to melatonin).

The primary function of GI melatonin is to strengthen our esophageal and gastric mucosal barriers, protecting them from inflammation and irritants, such as gastric acid, alcohol, and NSAIDs. Studies show that melatonin is highly protective to the esophagus from pepsin and HCl. Melatonin gently inhibits the secretion of HCl while stimulating the release of gastrin, increasing the contraction of the LES. And finally, melatonin is an important mediator of the gut-brain axis, having protective effects against stress-related damage to our GI tract. Over the years, researchers have found that people with peptic ulcers or GERD have lower melatonin levels than healthy individuals. Melatonin production decreases as we age, and there tend to be more complications from GERD in older people. Could there be a connection?

There have been two studies evaluating melatonin for GERD and one pilot study for the drug ramelteon—a prescription drug that binds to melatonin receptors. The first study was a head-to-head single-blind comparison of patients with GERD split into two groups for a 40-day treatment period. In the first group, 175 patients received 20 mg per day of omeprazole (Prilosec™); in the second group, 176 patients received a supplement containing melatonin (6 mg), its precursor L-tryptophan, vitamins B6 and B12, folic acid, betaine, and methionine. All patients taking the melatonin combination reported *complete regression* of symptoms by the end of the study, compared to 66% in the omeprazole-treated group. While some patients receiving the melatonin combination reported drowsiness, both treatments were well-tolerated.

In 2010, a small and very well-done 8-week study randomized 27 patients with GERD into three groups: melatonin alone (3 mg fast-acting before bed), omeprazole alone (20 mg twice daily), or a combination of melatonin (3 mg fast acting before bed) plus omeprazole (20 mg twice daily). There were nine healthy age-matched controls. All patients underwent extensive history taking, clinical examination, and investigations, including endoscopic recording of esophageal motility, pH monitoring, and laboratory tests that included basal acid output and serum gastrin. Formal evaluations were conducted at 4 and 8 weeks.

At four weeks, the group receiving the combination of omeprazole and melatonin had *complete resolution* of their symptoms. By eight weeks, *all three treatment groups had complete resolution*. However, only the groups receiving melatonin *had a significant increase in LES tone* and a *significant decrease in the duration of transient LES relaxation*. This was a key and important finding, given that most of GERD is due to poor LES tone and gastric motility.

In 2016, a pilot study was conducted on ramelteon to evaluate its effectiveness in 16 people with heartburn and chronic insomnia. Extensive baseline information was gathered, including an upper endoscopy and pH testing. Participants were randomized to receive either 8 mg of ramelteon or placebo each night for four weeks. At the end of the study, the differences between the two groups were dramatic—those taking the ramelteon had a 42% reduction in nighttime and 24-hour heartburn. Those in the placebo group had no improvement in nighttime heartburn and only a 3% reduction in 24-hour heartburn. Sleep was also dramatically improved in the ramelteon group.

Melatonin is an incredibly effective tool for getting reflux under control. I've had tremendous success using it in patients with heartburn, particularly with nighttime symptoms. You will see that melatonin plays a central role in my protocols for those with mild-to-moderate GERD symptoms and as part of my tapering protocol for those taking PPIs. The safety of melatonin is excellent. For reflux, the dose is generally 3–6 mg taken for 2–4 months.

CHAPTER 6
Herbal Medicine for Reflux

I have long been an avid student of the natural world. I am deeply curious about how peoples have used plants, mushrooms, and seaweeds for food and medicine throughout time. I am also interested in how this historical knowledge holds up to modern scientific investigation. There are many plants that can have a beneficial impact upon the digestive tract. Herbal medicines can provide cost-effective and readily available gastro-protective remedies without significant side effects. While the title of this chapter is botanicals, I have included brown algae because of its amazing ability to help prevent reflux.

Demulcents: Gut Soothers

There are many plants (and algae) that can soothe and protect irritated tissues. Plants with this type of bioactivity are categorized as demulcents. Demulcents are generally rich in mucilage—or mucopolysaccharides—that become slippery and gelatinous when they contact water. They can form a protective barrier in our mouth, throat, esophagus, and stomach, helping to reduce cough and the harmful effects of gastric acid and other irritants. I will focus on those that have a strong historical use for heartburn (and other GI problems), are supported by modern science, and that I have found useful over the past four decades of practice. These include alginate (from algae), aloe vera, licorice, marshmallow, and slippery elm.

Alginate from Brown Algae

Examples of brown macroalgae include kelp, giant kelp (as pictured above), and bull kelp. Globally, brown algae are the most widely consumed algae and have been consumed as food for millennia. Even though brown algae can photosynthesize, have a holdfast (a structure that acts like a root), blades (leaves), and stipes (stems)—they are *not* plants. They are protists, a category defined mainly by what they are not, versus what they are: eukaryotic organisms that are not animals, plants, or fungi. Brown algae contain alginate (or alginic acid), a polysaccharide in their cell walls which helps give the algae flexibility and strength. Alginates act as prebiotics, promoting the growth of *Bifidobacterium bifidum*, *Bifidobacterium longum* and *Lactobacilli*, and inhibiting the growth of harmful bacteria; improving and restoring the health of the gut microbiome. This makes alginates incredibly important for our overall health but there's more to the story: they have been successfully used for decades to manage heartburn. Let me tell you how.

After eating a meal, an acid pocket forms on top of our stomach contents right below where our stomach joins our esophagus. With a pH of 2, if the LES relaxes, or you have a hiatal hernia, these highly acidic contents can reflux back up into the esophagus and throat, inflaming and irritating the tissue. The position of this acid pocket explains why GERD symptoms are often worse after eating, and when lying down—and this is where alginates play a crucial role. Upon contact with stomach acid, alginates form a strong and buoyant gel that floats on top of the acid pocket, creating a physical barrier between the pocket and the LES. This floating effect is why they are called "*raft* forming" alginates. Displacing the acid pocket is a useful and safe strategy for relieving and preventing GERD, as it is a physical, not pharmacologic intervention. Alginates also act as a bioadhesive, adhering to the esophageal mucosa and protecting it against acid reflux for up to one hour after eating. Relief is often rapid.

There have been numerous studies showing that alginates can be highly effective for relieving acid reflux. A 2017 systematic review found that alginates are superior to antacids for improving GERD symptoms (either complete resolution or significant improvement) and just a little less effective than PPIs. The reviewers concluded that "*available clinical trials support the efficacy of alginates for the treatment of symptomatic GERD.*"

I use alginates for treating GERD, to help wean people off PPIs, and for restoring and strengthening the gut microbiome.

Dose: 500–1,000 mg taken after meals, as needed. This is an excellent recommendation for those with mild-to-moderate GERD and to relieve break-through heartburn during tapering protocols.

Safety: Alginates are very well tolerated and have an excellent safety profile.

Aloe Vera Gel (*Aloe Vera* (L.) Webb.)

When I opened my first herbal clinic in Las Cruces, NM, locals often came in looking to purchase aloe vera gel by the gallon. When I asked why they drank so much of it, invariably, they would say, "*Ayuda a mi estomago,*"—it helps my stomach. Over the past forty years, I have come to understand why so many sang its praises. Not only does it offer incredible healing for the skin, but it is also a truly wondrous herb for soothing the mouth, throat, esophagus, stomach, and small intestine while easing gas, bloating, and heartburn. I have been thrilled to see the growing number of aloe drinks in the marketplace.

Aloe vera is a hardy succulent with spear-like leaves and has been used in medicine for millennia. There are more than 150 different species and varieties of aloe. Native originally to the Arabian Peninsula, aloe is now naturalized and cultivated in many parts of the world. It has been brokered and traded for more than 5,000 years. It is known as the plant of immortality in Egypt and was treasured by Greek and Roman physicians for its ability to protect the skin, heal wounds, and ease digestive woes.

The aloe vera leaf is made up of an outer green rind and an inner gel. The inner gel contains two main liquids. Just under the rind is a bitter yellow latex called aloe juice or sap, and then there is a clear, sticky, mucilaginous gel in the inner leaf. The bitter yellow latex is a potent laxative due to the presence of anthraquinones (e.g., aloin A, aloin B) and should be avoided or used only occasionally if needed. These anthraquinone compounds can be readily removed in a process called decolorization. We are only interested in the *decolorized aloe vera inner leaf gel* for this discussion on reflux.

Aloe vera inner leaf gel is made up primarily of polysaccharides and water. Acemannan is the dominant polysaccharide in the gel and has been shown to have beneficial effects on both our immune and GI systems. Modern science confirms that aloe vera has potent anti-inflammatory, anti-ulcer, wound-healing, and antimicrobial activity, and profound gastroprotective effects. It effectively lowers gastric acid secretion and increases mucin production in the small intestine, helping protect the duodenum from injury.

Can aloe vera gel help with reflux? The answer is yes. A 2015 study randomized 79 people diagnosed with GERD by endoscopy into three groups: 10 ml of aloe vera syrup per day (standardized to 5 mg polysaccharide per mL of syrup), omeprazole 20 mg per day, or the H2 blocker ranitidine 150 mg in the morning and 150 mg before bed. Patients were evaluated at baseline, 2 weeks, and again at 4 weeks. While the PPI was more effective for alleviating heartburn than aloe vera, aloe was equivalent for all other GERD related symptoms (e.g., food regurgitation, difficulty swallowing, flatulence, nausea, vomiting).

In addition to its benefit for reflux, aloe vera gel acts as a prebiotic; increasing levels of *Bifidobacterium* and *Lactobacilli* (friendly bacteria), stimulating the production of short-chained fatty acids necessary for the health of intestinal cells, enhancing mineral absorption, and reducing systemic inflammation. Give the dysbiosis that occurs with PPI treatment, this potent prebiotic effect is very beneficial for helping balance and restore the gut microbiota. This prebiotic effect may also explain aloe vera's beneficial effect in irritable bowel syndrome and overall intestinal health. And due to its anti-inflammatory nature, aloe vera has been found to increase remission and improve symptoms in people with ulcerative colitis.

I find aloe vera gel to be incredibly healing, soothing, and protective to the esophagus and stomach tissue.

Dose: The recommended amount of gel is generally 1–2 ounces or 10,000–20,000 mg pure aloe vera gel taken 1–2 times daily. Note: many dietary supplements contain concentrated aloe vera gel extracts. An example of a label might say: aloe vera inner leaf 100 mg (200:1), which is equivalent to 20,000 mg of pure aloe vera gel (100 mg x 200 = 20,000 mg).

Safety: Drinking or taking soft gel capsules of aloe vera gel that is *aloin-free* is quite safe. All the risks you read about for aloe vera are for the "whole leaf" extract. Make sure you look for a product that only uses the *"inner leaf."* Always check labels carefully to ensure the product you are recommending is aloin-free, as anthraquinones can increase the risk of colon cancer when taken long-term.

Licorice Root (*Glycyrrhiza glabra, G. uralensis* Fisch. ex. DC.)

Once I was asked which 12 herbal medicines I would want to have if I was stranded on a desert island. Thought-provoking. Licorice root definitely made my short list. That's because over the past four decades, I have found it to be one of the most versatile herbal medicines. I include it in formulations for oral, respiratory, gastrointestinal, and skin problems. It is a potent anti-inflammatory, soothing to the throat, esophagus, and stomach tissue. Licorice is an excellent expectorant, thinning mucus and making it easier to expel from the lungs. It is anti-tussive, meaning it is highly effective for easing coughs. It is included in creams for soothing rashes and eczema, and frequent application of licorice tincture at the first sign of a cold sore can often abort an eruption entirely. I think you can see why I'm a fan.

Licorice root has been used to soothe irritation and halt inflammation for more than 3,000 years. The gastro-protectant effects have been recognized for centuries. Licorice root was mainstream medicine's treatment of choice for healing gastric ulcers up through the 1950s. Germany's health authorities still endorse the use of licorice root for gastric and duodenal ulcers and based upon long-standing traditional use, the European Medicines Agency endorses the use of licorice the relief of digestive symptoms including burning sensations and dyspepsia.

Research shows licorice is an effective anti-ulcer agent, similar in efficacy to the H2 blocker famotidine. Licorice raises the local concentration of prostaglandins that promote mucus secretion in the stomach, leading to the healing of ulcers. Unfortunately, nearly one in five people who were treated with licorice for their ulcers, developed high blood pressure and had a dangerous drop in their potassium after using high doses of licorice root for several months. While 80% of people did just fine on this higher, prolonged dose of licorice, it is concerning that 20% did not. Why?

There are many active compounds in licorice including more than 300 flavonoids and 20 terpenes. One of these compounds, glycyrrhizin, is what causes the body to retain sodium, lose potassium, and elevate blood pressure over time. A special preparation—deglycyrrhizinated licorice (DGL)—has had 98–99% of the glycyrrhizin removed, making it safe to take long-term. DGL is gastroprotective, has antibacterial and antiadhesive activity to *H. pylori*, and beneficial effects on gastric motility. When you put it all together, it makes a great option for those looking to manage their reflux or wean off PPIs.

Dose: Chew 1– 2 tablets (380–760 mg) DGL, or take an equivalent amount in liquid form, before or immediately after meals for relief of heartburn. Because DGL has had 98–99% of the glycyrrhizin removed, it safe to take for long periods.

Safety: Do not take licorice root if you have high blood pressure, heart or kidney disease, or low blood potassium. The European monograph states that 100 mg of the compound glycyrrhizin is not likely to cause adverse effects in most people. Given that glycyrrhizin is present at 4–9% in the root, 1,000 mg/d of licorice is likely safe in otherwise healthy people (40–90 mg of glycyrrhizin per day). DGL is however, your safest choice.

Marshmallow Leaf/Root (*Althaea officinalis* L.)

Marshmallow is one of my favorite herbs. I grow it in my garden and harvest the leaves in the summer and the roots in autumn when the plants are 2–3 years old. Both the leaves and roots are rich in mucilage (roughly 6–10%), making them excellent for soothing coughs, sore throats, and heartburn. At one of my classes held on our ranch in northern New Mexico, I had students help me harvest marshmallow and prepare tea and syrup from it. The natural taste is pleasant, and with a little vanilla extract, it is divine. One of my students, an emergency room physician, later told me that he struggled with occasional heartburn for years and had never found anything as effective as drinking marshmallow tea. He was so surprised and delighted. I was also delighted but not surprised. This plant has been an ally of mine for more than 40 years.

And yes, the name of this plant is the same as the sweet confectionary many of us roast over campfires, usually squished between a graham cracker and a piece of chocolate! This kind of sweet treat is said to have originated over 2,000 years ago in Egypt, where marshmallow root was powdered and then blended with honey as a treat for royalty and offering to the gods. Later in Europe, physicians and pharmacists would blend the powdered marshmallow root with egg whites, sugar, and other ingredients to create a tasty treat that could soothe coughs and digestive irritation in the young and old. Unfortunately, modern marshmallows are loaded in sugar and contain none of the herb.

This beautiful member of the rose family has been used as both food and medicine since ancient times. Historically, marshmallow was used for inflammation of the respiratory, urinary, and gastrointestinal systems. The mucilage and other compounds in marshmallow protect the tissues that line the throat, esophagus, and stomach, reducing and relieving inflammation and irritation. This is not only due to its ability to "coat" the tissue but also by stimulating local prostaglandins, which increase the stomach's production of mucin (mucus), the body's natural protection against the highly acidic environment of the stomach. This is great for GERD and particularly beneficial for those with laryngeal esophageal reflux due to its ability to alleviate cough. Finally, marshmallow root contains small amounts of pectin—a dietary fiber also found in apples—that acts as a prebiotic, promoting a healthy gut microbiota.

Most of the clinical research on marshmallow has been on its beneficial use in cough, for which the studies are highly favorable. The evidence for its use in acid reflux is primarily pre-clinical. However, when we look at what other expert bodies say about marshmallow root, we find that the German health authorities and Health Canada endorse its use for mild inflammation of the gastric mucosa, and the European Union monograph recognizes the traditional use of marshmallow root for the symptomatic relief of mild gastrointestinal discomfort. Going further, the British Herbal Compendium endorses the use of marshmallow root for the treatment of duodenal ulcers, ulcerative colitis, and digestive inflammation.

Dose: Marshmallow tea should be carefully prepared to prevent destroying the mucilage. One tsp. of dried root should be steeped in 8 ounces of room temperature water for 2–3 hours. Strain and drink. Repeat as needed. Marshmallow is also available in syrups that can be taken instead of tea. If taking in a liquid or syrup, look for those that provide 1,000 mg per serving.

Safety: Marshmallow root and leaf are both extremely safe. The European Union monograph states that up to 15 grams per day can be used, though, the dose is generally 1–3 grams per day taken in divided doses. Some experts recommend taking prescription medications 1 hour before, or 2 hours after, taking marshmallow root.

Slippery Elm Bark (*Ulmus rubra* Muhl.; syn. *Ulmus fulva* Michx)

I absolutely adore slippery elm bark. It is the inner, not the whole bark, that is used! I mix slippery elm bark powder with a little water to make a paste, and then add boiling water to make porridge when someone in the family has gastroenteritis (e.g., nausea and diarrhea). A little pumpkin pie spice and maple syrup before serving and, voilà, a hearty and soothing medicinal food! This modern version probably tastes better than the slippery elm bark porridge that kept George Washington and his soldiers alive at Valley Forge for 12 days when there was nothing else to eat.

In addition to its use as food, indigenous peoples and early settlers relied upon it to relieve coughs, sore throats and gastritis. It was cooked in lard and applied topically for the treatment of burns and boils. Poultices were applied to swollen glands and painful joints.

Slippery elm bark was an official drug in the United States Pharmacopeia (USP) from 1820–1936 as a demulcent and cough suppressant. Today, slippery elm bark is FDA approved as a safe and effective over-the-counter oral demulcent and it is once again official in the USP! Oral demulcents are approved for soothing irritated tissue of the mouth and throat, something deeply appreciated by professional singers and speakers. This also makes slippery elm helpful as an *adjunctive therapy* for LPR, where there is throat irritation due to acid reflux.

Like the other herbs mentioned in this section, the demulcent activity of slippery elm is due to the presence of mucopolysaccharides. In addition, research shows that slippery elm dramatically increases the abundance of butyrate producing intestinal bacteria, helping to reduce inflammation and improve the function of the intestinal barrier. With improved barrier function there is less circulating endotoxin, a well-known trigger of inflammation in the body. This impact on gut microbiota may explain the health generating benefits noted for many of the mucopolysaccharide rich plants.

Dose: 200–500 mg taken 2–6 times per day, or as needed. Slippery elm can be made as a tea, syrup, or lozenge. Capsules of slippery elm do not offer much protection for the esophagus.

Safety: Because it can coat the stomach, it is generally recommended to take prescription medications 1 hour before, or 2 hours after, taking slippery elm.

Note: Slippery elm trees are vulnerable to Dutch Elm disease. The United Plant Savers state, "due to the declining wild populations of *U. rubra* it is important to not use any wild-harvested bark unless harvested from naturally felled trees." Organically grown and cultivated slippery elm is most often used in commercial herbal preparations.

Prokinetics: Gut Movers

For healthy digestion to occur, the contracting and relaxing of muscles in your esophagus, stomach, and intestines (gastric motility) must be well-coordinated. When dysmotility occurs, heartburn, indigestion (dyspepsia), and/or irritable bowel syndrome often results. About 40% of patients with indigestion have delayed gastric emptying due to poor stomach motility. Food sits too long in their stomach, which causes distension, and often, acid reflux. Prokinetics are substances that quicken or speed up gastric or intestinal motility. Why don't we use these more in conventional medicine? Because most prescription prokinetics have significant side effects. Some have even been removed from the market.

Fortunately, Nature has provided us with several botanicals that act as prokinetics, including artichoke leaf, ginger rhizome, and Indian gooseberry to name a few. Additionally, magnesium can act as a prokinetic which I will cover in the chapter on micronutrients.

Globe Artichoke Leaf (*Carduus cardunculus var. scolymus L.*)

Who doesn't love to eat artichoke hearts? What a treat! Did you know that artichoke is a thistle in the Sunflower family, and the parts you eat are the young flower heads? The 'hearts' have long been a treasured delicacy. The ancient Egyptians, Greeks, and Romans used the leaves to ease heartburn, gas, bloating, and strengthen the liver. My first encounter with a "medicinal" artichoke was in Italy, where I was given a small glass of Cynar (chee-nar) after eating a rather heavy meal in Naples. Cynar is a liqueur made primarily from artichoke leaf, along with thirteen other herbs that round out the flavor. After about 20 minutes, I realized the bloating and accompanying "why did I eat so much" feeling was gone. I now use artichoke leaf, usually in combination with other herbs, to improve gut motility, assist in the digestion of fats, reduce reflux, and ease the symptoms of IBS. I use it in combination with milk thistle for promoting liver health. Artichoke is one of my go-to herbs for those who struggle with *heartburn and bloating, especially after eating fatty foods*!

Artichoke leaf increases bile secretion, which helps fat digestion and reduces bloating, nausea, and gas in human clinical trials. Also, artichoke leaves contain the prebiotic inulin, which increases *Bifidobacterium* levels, crucial to a healthy gut microbiome. These two effects help to explain why artichoke leaf is so good for easing indigestion and IBS. A randomized, double-blind, placebo-controlled study of 247 people with recurrent pain/discomfort in their upper abdomen and a diagnosis of functional dyspepsia found that artichoke leaf extract was highly effective for relieving fullness, flatulence, and early satiety. Another study of 208 adults with both dyspepsia and IBS, found that artichoke leaf extract significantly improved IBS symptoms and quality of life. And in a survey of ~300 people with IBS, 96% of participants rated artichoke leaf as superior or equivalent to other IBS treatments.

Artichoke leaf increases gastric motility, which is one reason it can be so beneficial as an after-dinner drink, like Cynara. As it helps move food through the digestive tract, artichoke leaf can reduce post-meal heartburn and indigestion. One study found the combination of ginger and artichoke leaf significantly promoted gastric emptying in healthy volunteers. Artichoke leaf also increases gastric mucus (mucin) secretion, which helps protect the stomach from the irritant effects of HCl, pepsin, and certain medications. For this reason, it has a long been used as a treatment for gastric ulcers.

Additionally, artichoke has a beneficial effect on lipids, acting in a milder but similar pathway as statin drugs. Research shows that it inhibits HMG-CoA reductase, interfering with the liver's ability to make cholesterol. While not as potent as prescription drugs, numerous studies confirm that artichoke leaf has mild cholesterol and triglyceride-lowering effects, making it a useful adjunct to lifestyle or drug therapy. Artichoke leaf has a protective effect on the liver by reducing inflammation and promoting the movement of bile. Preclinical research found that globe artichoke extract protected against liver injury due to acetaminophen overdose. In a clinical trial of 90 people with non-alcoholic fatty liver disease, artichoke leaf extract reduced the level of fat in the liver, while also reducing liver enzymes, indicating a liver-protecting effect.

Although the research is not yet conclusive, scientists believe that the long-standing use of artichoke leaf in humans for digestive problems is justified by both preclinical and human clinical trials. And it seems the European Medicines Agency agrees, stating that artichoke leaf preparations can be used for the relief of digestive disorders.

Dose: Generally, 300–600 mg of artichoke leaf extract is taken up to three times per day. I generally recommend it primarily after the "main meal" of the day. Quality products are often standardized to cynarin (3–5%), a major bioactive found in the leaf.

Safety: Because artichoke leaf can promote the flow of bile, one should use caution if they have a history of bile duct obstruction. While skin contact with the artichoke plant can cause allergic reactions in some people, there have not been any reports of allergic reaction from the oral ingestion of the leaf extract.

Note: Artichoke is known to activate "sweet" receptors in the mouth. Many wine experts are aware of this and discourage eating artichoke hearts when wine tasting as it makes everything taste sweeter than it really is. Just something to keep in mind when eating or using artichoke. Taking artichoke leaf *after* meals is good for the tummy and won't interfere with your taste buds during your dinner!

Ginger (*Zingiber officinale* Roscoe)

I can still remember the smell of gingerbread cookies baking in my grandma's kitchen at Christmas time. Yum! The aroma was heavenly. Whether it is ginger tea, grated fresh ginger in cooking, candied ginger, or cookies—I adore its warming, spicy flavor. Originating in southeast Asia, ginger is now grown in many tropical and subtropical areas of the world. In addition to its long history in food, it has also been a treasured medicine. Most of us know that ginger is excellent for relieving nausea and stomach upset, but it also great for coughs, colds, headaches, menstrual and intestinal cramping, enhancing circulation, and warming you down to your fingers and toes.

For the purposes of this chapter, I'll focus on the use of ginger for gastrointestinal problems. People have relied on the digestive relieving properties of ginger for more than 3,000 years. It's ability to ease heartburn and indigestion is one of the reasons it is so treasured as a spice in food dishes. As an anti-nausea aid, it is very effective for both motion and morning sickness. Even the American College of Obstetrics and Gynecology formally recommends taking 250 mg of dried ginger powdered capsules up to four times per day to ease the nausea and vomiting of pregnancy. The reason it so effectively reduces gas, bloating and heartburn is its ability to enhance gastric motility. It keeps food moving through the stomach which decreases the pressure on the LES. It also reduces intestinal cramping and stimulates the release of pancreatic lipase, aiding the digestion of fats.

A study randomized 24 volunteers with dyspepsia to take 3 ginger capsules (1,200 mg total) or placebo after an eight-hour fast. One hour later, participants were fed 500 ml of low-nutrient soup. The median gastric half emptying time was 2.3 min after ginger, versus 16.1 min after placebo. In other words, those who had taken ginger prior to the meal, experienced much faster transit through the stomach.

Dose: 500–1,200 mg dried ginger taken with or immediately after a meal. Ginger teabags are readily available and are a convenient and tasty way to take ginger after meals. Fresh ginger can also be used, usually at 2–3 times the dried dose.

Safety: There are no safety concerns with these doses of ginger in healthy adults. Pregnant women should not exceed 1,500 mg per day of dried ginger. Though it is often said that ginger decreases platelet aggregation, a pharmacokinetic study in healthy volunteers administered 1.2 grams three times per day and it failed to show any adverse effect on platelets or interference with warfarin.

Note: I love ginger for its ability to relieve gas and bloating but in my experience, higher doses of dried ginger (more than 2–3 grams) can actually increase heartburn and reflux. If you want to try ginger, start with a smaller amount (500–1,000 mg) and see how you feel.

Indian gooseberry (*Emblica officinalis Gaertn*; syn. *Phyllanthus emblica* L.)

Indian gooseberry, more commonly known as amla, is one of the oldest edible fruits in India and other subtropical regions of southern Asia, treasured as both food and medicine. These delightfully sour fruits are extremely high in vitamin C, polyphenols, and flavonoids, contributing to their overall nutritional value. Amalaki, one of its other names, means *"the sustainer,"* denoting its long history as one of Ayurveda's premier rejuvenating medicinal remedies. (Ayurveda is the traditional medical system of India.) Amla is one of the primary ingredients in Chyawanprash (chyavanaprasha), an Indian jam consumed to enhance vitality, restore vigor, and strengthen the digestive and immune systems. Amla is one of three fruits that make up Triphala (literally means, three fruits), a highly regarded Ayurvedic formulation used to regulate digestion and elimination, reduce hyperacidity, help maintain healthy blood sugar levels, and squelch inflammation.

Amla has long been used to ease sore throats, soothe inflammation in the gut, and ease indigestion. Science shows that amla fruits act as a prokinetic, strengthening the tone of the LES, decreasing reflux, and promoting the movement of food through the stomach. It is highly cyto-protective, meaning that it helps to prevent damage to the gastric and intestinal mucosa from irritants, whether gastric acid, medications or alcohol, by increasing local prostaglandins and mucus production. Numerous preclinical studies have shown that amla promotes the healing of gastric ulcers caused by taking NSAIDs.

Given all this goodness, are there any human clinical trials on amla and acid reflux? Yes! A four-week randomized double-blind, placebo-controlled clinical trial of 68 patients, experiencing symptoms of GERD for at least three months, received either 1,000 mg of amla twice daily after meals or similar looking placebo. The group receiving the amla had a more significant reduction in both regurgitation and heartburn frequency and severity, compared to placebo.

Dose: If taking the powder, start with 250–500 mg once a day and increase if needed. You can eat the fresh fruit if available. Chop and de-seed one cup of fresh gooseberries and put them in the blender. Add the juice from one lemon, 1 tsp. sugar, ¼ tsp. ginger powder, ¼ tsp cardamom, 1 cup of ice cubes, and a pinch of salt. Blend well and adjust to taste. You can drink ½ of this before lunch and dinner to aid digestion and ease heartburn.

Safety: No significant safety concerns. High doses (4 grams) can have a stool softening and laxative effect.

The Mind-Gut Connection

It is widely recognized that stress can worsen acid reflux. Stress decreases prostaglandins, involved in making mucus (mucin), which buffers stomach acid, as well as increasing stomach acid. It has been shown that those with high stress and/or anxiety have more severe reflux and more retrosternal pain. Luckily, there are herbs that can help soothe anxiety and stress, while also protecting the GI tract. One that stands out as being very effective for both is German chamomile.

German Chamomile Flowers (*Matricaria chamomilla* L. syn. *M. recutita* L.)

German chamomile is one of our most popular medicinal herbs, ranking among the top five selling herbs globally, and is cherished particularly for use in the young and old. The name chamomile comes from the Greek *chamos* (ground) and *melos* (apple), as it grows close to the earth and has a pleasant apple-like aroma. The aromatic chamomile flower has been a prized medicine for thousands of years; highly valued in Egyptian, Greek and Roman medicine. The Anglo Saxons considered it to be one of nine sacred herbs given to humans by God.

Because chamomile is gentle enough to use in young children, it is often overlooked when it comes to relieving tension and easing feelings of anxiety. But in an NIH-funded, randomized, double-blind study conducted at the University of Pennsylvania, chamomile extract was superior to placebo for reducing anxiety symptoms in patients diagnosed with generalized anxiety disorder (GAD) after 12 weeks of use. In a 26-week follow-up, chamomile continued to significantly and safely reduce symptoms of GAD. There were also no significant differences between placebo and chamomile extract with regards to adverse effects.

Science confirms that chamomile has anti-inflammatory, antispasmodic, relaxant, and antiseptic activity. It is commonly consumed in tea to relieve abdominal pain, sluggish digestion, flatulence, and nausea. The European Medicines Agency has concluded that, based upon its long-standing use, chamomile can treat the symptoms of minor gastrointestinal complaints such as bloating and spasms. The German health authorities recognize the benefit of chamomile to help relieve inflammatory conditions of the GI tract, to help relieve mild digestive disturbances (e.g., dyspepsia, gassiness, bloating), and as a calmative and/or sleep aid.

Research shows that chamomile increases mucin secretion in the stomach and mildly inhibits stomach acid production. This relaxes the fundus and increases antral contractility in the stomach, which reduces feelings of distension and allows food to move more quickly into the intestine. All of these effects are beneficial for those struggling with acid reflux.

Dose: 1,000 mg taken 1–3 times per day. Chamomile is widely available in teabags and capsules.

Safety: Chamomile is considered quite safe and is widely consumed worldwide by infants, children, adults, and elders alike. It is a member of the Asteraceae family, so those with severe allergies to ragweed should exercise some caution with its use.

Mastic Gum (*Pistacia lentiscus* L.)

I find tree resins fascinating. I harvest pine resin for use in ointments as all tree resins are strong antibacterial agents, and most are excellent for healing wounds, inside and out. After being injured by pests, trees secrete resin/sap to protect and heal their wounds. Resin from the stem of the mastic tree is known as mastic gum, and the most prized mastic gum comes from the island of Chios, where it is known as the "tears of Chios." Chios mastic gum is harvested and prepared the same way today as it has been for thousands of years, prompting UNESCO to put it on its List of Intangible Cultural Heritage.

In Greek, mastic means to *"to gnash the teeth."* Considered by many to be the world's first chewing gum, mastic gum was also used to clean teeth and improve bad breath. And modern science has confirmed that mastic gum is active against numerous oral pathogens that cause periodontal disease. For more than 2,500 years, physicians and healers have used mastic gum to treat gastric pain, dyspepsia and peptic ulcers. Today, chewing gum is still recommended for those with heartburn, as it stimulates salivation, which dilutes stomach acid and helps to wash acid from the esophagus back into the stomach. Those ancients knew a thing or two, didn't they?

Mastic gum contains numerous compounds with anti-inflammatory, antioxidant, anti-ulcer properties, and potent antibacterial activity against multiple pathogens, including *H. pylori.* Researchers found that 9 of 26 participants successfully cleared *H. pylori* after chewing pure mastic gum for two weeks; however, those who took an antibiotic *plus* mastic gum saw the highest success rate (10 or 13 participants). That suggests mastic gum could be useful as an *adjunctive* treatment to standard care for *H. pylori* eradication. More research on herbal medicines that could help to eradicate *H. pylori* is important given its strong relationship to stomach ulcers, gastric cancer, and the growing resistance to antibiotics.

Mastic gum has significant gastro-protective properties. As mentioned previously, stress can be a significant cause of gastritis. In preclinical research, when given prior to a stressor, mastic gum protected the gastric and intestinal mucosa with similar efficacy to the PPI omeprazole. In fact, one older study of 38 patients with duodenal ulcer found that 70% of patients taking 1 gram/day of mastic gum had endoscopically proven healing, compared to 22% of patients taking placebo. Mastic gum mildly reduces gastric acid while being a potent stimulant for mucin production, especially in those who are anxious or stressed. A randomized, double-blind, placebo-controlled study of 148 patients evaluated the effectiveness of 350 mg of mastic gum taken three times daily against placebo for relieving the symptoms of functional dyspepsia (e.g., gas, bloating, heartburn). There was a marked improvement of symptoms in 77% of patients receiving mastic gum compared to 40% taking placebo. Individual symptoms that showed a statistically significant improvement with mastic gum were stomach pain in general, but particularly when anxious, dull ache in the upper abdomen, and heartburn.

Dose: The dose varies from 100–350 mg taken 1 to 3 times daily. It is available as chewing gum, in capsules and delivered in liquid. There are also mastic gum toothpastes and mouthwashes that can be useful for controlling dental plaque.

Safety: Mastic gum appears to be quite safe in the amounts being recommended. With higher dosing, diarrhea can occur. There *may be* cross-reactivity in those who have an allergy to pistachio or tree nuts.

CHAPTER 7

Digestive Enzymes and Betaine HCl

As a physician, I have found that many people report better digestion while using digestive enzymes and/or betaine HCl supplements. Years ago, when my parents came to visit, my father was having difficulty with his digestion; heartburn, bloating, feeling full early in his meals. He was in his mid-70s at the time and had undergone chemotherapy for his prostate cancer. He believed that affected his digestion. I gave him a broad-spectrum digestive enzyme supplement that would aid in digesting protein, fats, carbohydrates, lactose, beans, and vegetables. I had him take them before every meal during their stay. Within just a few days, he experienced incredible relief, no longer leaving the table in the middle of dinner or endlessly excusing himself for passing gas.

Years later, he underwent chemotherapy again due to the progression of his prostate cancer. He was placed on a PPI and told to discontinue his digestive enzymes. After being left on the PPI for several years, he was treated for C. *difficile* and months later, hospitalized for severe hypomagnesemia and found to be vitamin B12 deficient. At that point, his doctors discontinued the PPI, but he began experiencing heartburn and bloating again. He went back on his digestive enzymes but didn't think they were working. I switched him over to betaine HCl, which dramatically reduced his heartburn and bloating within days. While it might seem counterintuitive to give HCl to someone with acid reflux, I knew that a man in his 80s *did not have excess stomach acid*; he didn't have enough. And while the pancreas releases enzymes into the small bowel that aid in the digestion of macronutrients, there is a natural decline in pancreatic enzymes as we age. *Incomplete digestion* can be the cause of acid reflux in some individuals.

Digestive Enzymes

Our gastrointestinal system (e.g., salivary glands, stomach, pancreas, small intestine) secretes digestive enzymes to break down proteins (proteases), fats (lipases), and carbohydrates (amylases) for nutrients to be absorbed. People taking PPIs often complain of abdominal pain, gas, and bloating. Digestive enzyme supplementation can often relieve these dyspeptic symptoms. A study of patients diagnosed with inflammatory bowel disease or irritable bowel syndrome found that when digestive enzymes were added to conventional treatment, there was a greater reduction in abdominal pain, bloating, and gas.

HCl produced in the stomach activates pepsin, the key enzyme required for protein digestion. When stomach acid shuts down, protein digestion is impaired. When gastric pH increases (gets less acidic), so does the risk for sensitization to food allergens. Gastric acid decreases the potential of food proteins to bind IgE antibodies, which increases the level of allergens required to elicit symptoms in someone with food allergies. As I mentioned earlier, food allergies are a rising concern in the Western world; could protease and/or HCl supplements help someone taking PPIs long-term, reduce this risk? The answer is: we don't know but it is a hypothesis that should be studied.

Several plants contain proteolytic enzymes (protease, protein-digesting), which aid digestion. Three of which, pineapple, papaya, and kiwifruit, are well-researched and widely used in traditional medicine.

- **Pineapple** fruit (and stem) contain a group of proteolytic enzymes known as bromelain. The fruit/bromelain aids digestion, eases cough, and loosens mucus. It also has potent anti-inflammatory activity which helps to ease the pain of arthritis and sports injuries.

- **Papaya fruit** (and leaf) contains papain and chymopapain, two proteolytic enzymes, shown to increase intestinal motility and have antiviral and antibacterial activity. Research also shows papaya can alleviate constipation, gas, and bloating.
- **Kiwifruit** contains the proteolytic enzyme actinidin. Kiwifruit and actinidin increase gastric emptying and enhance gastric digestion of food proteins, particularly those found in yogurt, cheese, fish, eggs, and gluten. Kiwifruit moves food more quickly through the intestine, easing constipation.

Adding these fruits to the diet can aid protein digestion, as well as offer other benefits. However, these plant-based enzymes are also available in dietary supplements, often in combination with other enzymes. Digestive enzymes can also be microbial-derived or animal-derived.

Tips for Using Digestive Enzymes

- Look for a product with proteases designed to work across varying pH (pH of 3–6), especially if taking a PPI.

- **Bromelain and papain** are good choices for proteases. If allergic to pineapple or papaya, do not use. Do not use these proteases if you are taking medications to prevent blood clotting (e.g., warfarin, Plavix). Do not use proteases if you have a history of gastric ulcers.

- If struggling with gas and bloating, in addition to heartburn, using a **broad-spectrum** digestive enzyme that helps digest carbohydrates (e.g., amylase), fats (e.g., lipase), lactose (e.g., lactase), and proteins (e.g., protease, bromelain, papain) might be your best option.

- **Dose:** Since products vary greatly, follow label instructions carefully.

Betaine HCl

What about HCl for someone taking a PPI? Now that sounds counterintuitive. Isn't the purpose of taking a PPI to shut down acid? Well, I spent a lot of time outlining problems with the long-term use of PPI medications. One possible way to reduce some of those adverse consequences is to drop the pH for a short while every day to activate pepsin and turn down gastrin to enhance the absorption of B12 and other essential vitamins and minerals.

It turns out a pilot study found that taking 1,500 mg of betaine HCl with 6 ounces of water right before a meal significantly and safely reduced gastric pH in healthy participants taking PPI medications by over 4 pH units, lowering gastric pH from above pH 5 to below pH 1 within ~6 minutes and lasting for more than a little more than one hour. Ideal if you think about it. Only effective for about one hour, long enough to do everything I just mentioned but not long enough to aggravate reflux. Taking supplemental betaine HCl with the main meal of the day may be safe and appropriate (and necessary) in people taking PPIs long-term to decrease side-effects (e.g., protein/micronutrient/drug malabsorption, food-borne pathogens, or slow gastric emptying).

It is very important to note that the research found that betaine HCl acts very quickly, so one should *only* take it *immediately before* a meal, and the *meal must contain protein*. Remember, HCl activates pepsin, which is the key enzyme for digesting protein. Do not take betaine HCl if your meal contains very little protein. I believe betaine HCl should be taken in partnership with your practitioner. I have included a *Clinician Directed Protocol for Betaine HCl* in Appendix 1.

Also, it is very important to note:

- The supplement is betaine HCl. Betaine is a compound naturally found in beets, spinach, wheat bran, and other foods, and is safe.
- Do not confuse betaine HCl with betaine trimethylglycine (TMG). These are two very different compounds and are used for different purposes.
- Betaine HCl must be taken in a tablet or capsule to avoid the HCl from coming into contact with your esophagus. Do not open a capsule and pour onto food or in liquid.
- Betaine HCl is contraindicated in those with peptic ulcer disease (now or in the past). Remember, never take this supplement on an empty stomach unless followed immediately by a protein-containing meal.

CHAPTER 8
Probiotics, Prebiotics, and Synbiotics

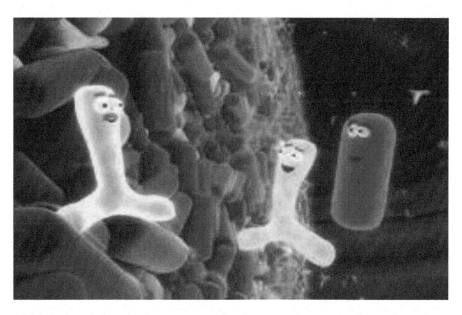

The gut microbiota plays a critical role in extracting and synthesizing vitamins and other nutrients from food; regulating digestion, metabolism, and elimination; fine-tuning the immune system; preventing the overgrowth of harmful bacteria; and maintaining the integrity and barrier function of the intestinal mucosa. Dysbiosis is a shift in the delicate balance between beneficial and pathogenic intestinal microorganisms and is shown to occur secondary to PPI use. While it is unclear if long-term PPI use increases the risk of gastric cancer, we know that low stomach acid reduces microbial diversity and increases the growth of bacteria with nitrate/nitrite reductase functions often involved in cancer development. Gastric dysbiosis is also very common in those with *H. pylori* infection, a major cause of gastric cancer—more on this later.

Probiotics are defined as "non-pathogenic living microorganisms that can colonize the intestinal tract and promote microbiota restoration, conferring a health benefit on the host when ingested in adequate amounts." *Lactobacillus* and *Bifidobacterium* species are most reportedly used as probiotics, but *Bacillus* species, and the nonpathogenic yeast *Saccharomyces cerevisiae,* are also used as probiotics. Prebiotics are substances that favor the growth of beneficial bacteria over harmful ones. Examples of prebiotics include oligofructose, inulin, and galacto-oligosaccharides. Many of the botanicals, as well as brown algae, mentioned in Chapter 6 are prebiotics. Synbiotics are a combination of probiotics and prebiotics. Researchers are increasingly looking at how these substances can support a healthy gut microbiota and improve quality of life, particularly in those taking PPIs.

A review of 13 prospective human clinical trials found that most studies reported positive outcomes for probiotics regarding GERD symptoms, reducing the number and frequency of reflux episodes. Probiotics accelerate gastric emptying, which may explain, in part, their beneficial effect on reflux symptoms. They also compete with other bacteria in the stomach, helping to reduce bacterial overgrowth. Additionally, probiotics have been shown to enhance the effectiveness of antibiotics in eradicating the *H. pylori* infection. Studies also show *Lactobacillus reuteri* and *Lactobacillus gasseri,* taken with PPIs but without antibiotics, can eliminate *H. pylori* infections.

PPI-induced dysbiosis is a subset of SIBO, often treated with minimally absorbed antibiotics (such as rifaximin). However, there is also a significant body of evidence that probiotics can also treat SIBO. A 2017 meta-analysis of 18 controlled studies found that probiotics can be effective in the treatment of SIBO, while a 2018 study found the combination of *Saccharomyces boulardii, Bifidobacterium lactis, Lactobacillus acidophilus,* and *Lactobacillus plantarum* dramatically improved symptoms in those with SIBO.

Could dysbiosis and SIBO be prevented by adding a prescription for probiotics with every prescription for a PPI? The answer appears to be yes based upon a wonderfully done study of 128 children with GERD. Researchers randomized the children to receive 12 weeks of PPIs (esomeprazole 1 mg/kg daily, once per day, maximum 40 mg) plus either a probiotic (*Lactobacillus reuteri* DM 17938) or placebo. The control group consisted of 120 healthy age-matched children. After 12 weeks, **dysbiosis occurred in 56.2% of the group receiving PPI + placebo** versus **only 6.2% of those taking the PPI + probiotics**. The risk for SIBO/dysbiosis from PPIs was dramatically reduced by adding this probiotic strain.

A similar result was found in an eight-week study of 134 adults with reflux esophagitis. Participants were placed on esomeprazole (20 mg twice daily) plus a probiotic (*Bacillus subtilis* and *Enterococcus faecium*) or placebo. While the healing rates between the groups were similar, there was significantly less SIBO, diarrhea, and abdominal discomfort in the group taking the PPI + probiotic, compared to placebo.

This improvement in quality of life was also found in a 2015 double-blind, placebo-controlled study of adults with GERD taking 40 mg per day of pantoprazole, randomized to receive the probiotic *Lactobacillus paracasei* F19 or placebo. The group taking probiotics had improved stool frequency and form with less flatulence and bloating compared to those taking placebo. Like the previous one, this study suggests that co-administration of probiotics can be very beneficial for minimizing these all too common and unpleasant symptoms people experience when taking a PPI.

As mentioned previously, in 2012, the FDA issued safety warnings for the potential increased risk of *C. difficile* infection associated with PPI therapy; yet another reason to consider probiotics, as they can reverse the overgrowth of pathogenic bacteria in the gut. A 2017 Cochrane review of 31 randomized controlled trials found that probiotics effectively prevent *C. difficile* associated diarrhea in both adults and children. And in 2018, a systematic review of clinical studies found that *Lactobacillus casei* and *L. rhamnosus* GG effectively prevented antibiotic-associated diarrhea and *C. difficile* infection. Personally, I feel there is more than enough research to support recommending specific probiotic strains to prevent dysbiosis and SIBO in people newly prescribed PPIs, *and* for people who must take PPIs long-term, reducing their risk for *C. diff* and other GI infections.

Which Kind: It is extremely important to use a high-quality probiotic product containing strains that have been studied in clinical trials. Different strains have different effects. Just like one antibiotic won't treat every type of infection, there is not a single probiotic strain that works for everything. The website usprobioticguide.com can be extremely helpful for finding the right product for you. I provide more instructions in the Resources section of the book.

Dose: The dose varies significantly between different probiotic strains. A great resource for determining which brand and how much to take can be found at the usprobioticguide.com website. You can filter by *H. pylori* eradication, prevention of *C. difficile*, functional abdominal pain, etc.

Safety: High-quality probiotics, prebiotics, and synbiotics have an excellent safety profile but you should not use them without the advice of your health care professional if you are immune-compromised or critically ill.

CHAPTER 9

Micronutrients to Consider

Gastric acid secretion is necessary to digest and absorb B12, iron, calcium, and probably magnesium. It is also essential to absorb, secrete, and activate ascorbic acid (vitamin C). Deficiencies in these essential nutrients can occur with prolonged PPI use due to decreased absorption or destruction secondary to bacterial overgrowth. Let's take a few minutes to discuss those of greatest concern if you are taking acid suppressing medications. Some of these are also highly relevant as we age due to the natural decline in stomach acid production that occurs.

The Minerals

Calcium

Calcium—in conjunction with vitamins D and K, magnesium, potassium, and other trace minerals—is vitally important for bone health. Calcium also plays important roles in nerve transmission, muscle contraction, and numerous enzymatic reactions. Gastric acid is necessary for increasing the dissolution and ionization of calcium salts (e.g., calcium carbonate), preparing it for absorption in the small intestine. When the FDA mandated a warning on PPI labels stating they can increase the risk for fracture, it was thought that this may be due, in part, to their effect on calcium. It is important to get adequate amounts of calcium rich foods in your diet. While dairy foods (e.g., cheese, yogurt, milk) provide most of the calcium in the American diet, ample supplies are also found in vegetables such as broccoli, cabbage, mustard, and collard greens. Dried apricots, almonds, and sardines are also good sources of absorbable calcium, as are some soy foods, and some fortified dairy alternative "milks" and juices.

Deficiency Signs & Symptoms: Often one of the first signs of calcium deficiency is muscle cramping and muscle ache. Many other signs—such as numbness or tingling of the fingers, poor appetite, and fatigue—are fairly nonspecific and could indicate a host of things.

Which Kind: Calcium citrate or malate is your best bet, especially if you are taking a PPI or are over age 50, as stomach acid is not required for absorption. Calcium carbonate requires an acidic environment for absorption, which makes it less optimal if you are taking acid suppressants. Calcium carbonate can act as a buffering agent, however, reducing acidity in the stomach, which is why it is FDA approved for the occasional treatment of heartburn.

Dose: Most healthy adults need ~1,000 mg per day, while everyone over age 70, and women after menopause, should strive for 1,200 mg per day. Do a rough calculation of what you are getting in your diet, and then supplement *only* the difference. For instance, if you are getting 650 mg in your diet, either up the amount of calcium rich foods or take a calcium citrate supplement that provides 300–400 mg per day. Your body cannot absorb more than 500–600 mg of calcium at a time, so if you have to take more, make sure it is in divided doses.

Safety: The upper tolerable limit for calcium from food and supplementation is 2,000 mg per day for those over age 50, and 2,500 mg per day for those 18–49 years old. Excessive calcium intake may be associated with heart disease, kidney stones, prostate cancer, and an increased risk of fracture. Some find that calcium supplements make them gassy or constipated, though this is more common with calcium carbonate. Taking your calcium with magnesium often improves these side effects. Calcium supplements should not be taken within 3–4 hours of certain medications (e.g., bisphosphonates, thyroid, etc.)

Iron

Over 60% of our body's iron is found in hemoglobin, the protein in our blood that carries oxygen from our lungs to our cells. Also, iron makes up part of our myoglobin, a protein that ensures enough oxygen is available to hard-working muscles. We need iron to make DNA, red blood cells, and energy production for normal development, reproduction, immune function, and detoxification. Unfortunately, according to the World Health Organization, iron deficiency is the most common deficiency in the world, affecting roughly 1.6 billion people

There are two forms of dietary iron: heme iron (~38% of our diet), from animals, and non-heme iron (~62% of our diet) from plants. Heme iron is bioavailable once it is acted upon by pancreatic enzymes in our small intestine. Non-heme iron is bound to vegetables, beans, and cereals and requires *gastric acid* to increase its bioavailability. Vitamin C helps increase non-heme iron absorption, but PPIs also decrease vitamin C levels in gastric juice. Studies show that multi-year use of PPIs can lower iron stores in our body, often requiring parenteral iron to correct the resulting iron deficiency anemia (IDA). In fact, PPIs have been used to treat people with hereditary hemochromatosis, a genetic condition that causes one's body to store excessive amounts of iron. Usually, these individuals are treated with phlebotomy (removing/donating blood) to remove the excess iron, but studies have found that PPIs can dramatically reduce their elevated iron levels. That's great if you have too much iron but can pose a real problem for those on long-term PPIs if no one is monitoring their iron status.

Deficiency Signs & Symptoms: Some symptoms of iron deficiency include fatigue, weak and/or rapid heart rate, heart palpitations, and an inability to get warm after exposure to the cold. Fingernails can become brittle and spoon shaped. Loss of taste and sore tongue can also occur.

Which Kind: There are numerous sources of iron supplements on the market. Most cause significant gastrointestinal distress, and for this reason, compliance is poor. An 8-week study conducted at the University of Maryland found a low-potency food-based iron was highly effective in raising iron levels without any adverse GI effects (Blood Builder®/Iron Response® by MegaFood).

Dose: If you have iron deficiency anemia, follow the instructions given by your health care provider. In general, only menstruating and pregnant women should routinely take iron supplements, or a multivitamin containing iron. If you are on long-term PPIs, make sure you ask your health care provider to order basic iron tests to determine if you need additional iron. The following is the recommended daily allowance (RDA) by gender.

- Men (all adult ages): 8 mg/day
- Women (19–50 years): 18 mg/day
- Women (19–50 years, pregnant): 27 mg/day
- Women (after 50 years): 8 mg

Note: The RDA for vegetarians is 1.8 times higher than for those who include meat/poultry/fish in their diets.

Safety: The tolerable upper limit is 45 mg per day of iron. Do NOT exceed this upper limit. Excess iron can be toxic as our bodies have no easy way of eliminating it. Excess iron can cause cirrhosis of the liver, diabetes, and heart failure. This upper limit does not pertain to those being treated for IDA by their health care professional.

Magnesium

Magnesium is the fourth most abundant mineral in our body, involved in more than 300 enzymatic reactions and playing a critical role in both DNA and RNA synthesis. Magnesium protects our cardiovascular system, maintaining healthy blood pressure and heart rhythm. Studies show that low magnesium levels are associated with an increased risk of dying from both coronary heart disease and sudden cardiac death. Magnesium is necessary for blood sugar regulation and the proper function of insulin. So, it should not be surprising to learn that one-third of those with type-2 diabetes are also magnesium deficient. While we discussed the relationship between PPIs, calcium and fracture, low magnesium also contributes to osteoporosis. A double whammy for our bones.

When all of this is considered, it is concerning that the FDA mandated a warning on PPI medications stating they can cause magnesium levels to fall dangerously low. This in the background of widespread insufficiency: surveys show that around 45% of Americans are magnesium deficient, and 60% of adults don't meet the recommended dietary intake.

Magnesium is found in both plant and animal foods. Cooked spinach, black beans, pumpkin seeds, almonds, cashews, soy milk, peanut butter, avocados, whole wheat bread, brown rice, yogurt, salmon, and milk are all excellent sources of magnesium. Of course, my favorite source is dark chocolate! Make sure that your diet contains adequate amounts of protein. When protein intake is less than 30 grams per day (equivalent to three ounces of red meat or one cup of cooked beans), magnesium absorption falls.

Deficiency Signs & Symptoms: The most common signs and symptoms include muscle cramps, twitching, and weakness; depression, apathy, fatigue, osteoporosis, elevated blood pressure and irregular heartbeat.

Which Kind: Magnesium malate, citrate, and glycinate are probably your best choices. Magnesium malate is highly absorbable and can reduce nocturnal reflux when taken before bed. Magnesium oxide is widely available but can be quite harsh on the GI tract, often causing diarrhea.

Dose: Supplementing with 300–400 mg of magnesium per day is suitable for most people. If you are taking PPIs and have any symptoms of low magnesium, you should ask your health care provider to check your magnesium levels, as you will likely require a higher dose to correct a deficiency.

Safety: Those with poor kidney function have more difficultly excreting excess magnesium and should check with their health care professional before taking supplemental magnesium. Magnesium can act as a laxative. Magnesium oxide is the worst offender. If diarrhea occurs, reduce your dose. Magnesium, like calcium, should be taken one hour before or two hours after taking other medications.

VITAMINS

Vitamin B12

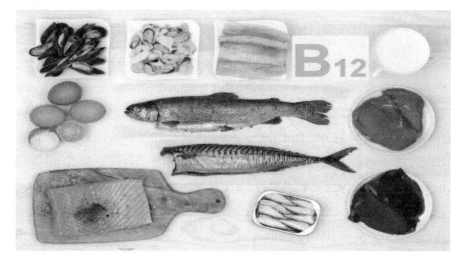

Vitamin B12 is necessary for physical and mental energy as well as emotional well-being. Along with B6 and folate, it plays an important role in the production of serotonin, dopamine, and norepinephrine, chemicals responsible for mood, pleasure, metabolism, stress response, and much more. Vitamin B12 helps produce myelin, the protective sheath that surrounds our nerves, explaining why a deficiency can cause tingling and burning in our arms and legs. B12 is also important for the functioning of our red and white blood cells, and a deficiency can cause anemia and diminished immune response.

The risk of vitamin B12 deficiency increases with age. According to data from the National Health and Nutrition Examination Survey (NHANES), 6.9% of adults aged 51–70 years and 15% of those over 70 years, are B12 deficient. Similar findings were reported in Germany, with 27.3% of people aged 65–93 years having very low B12 levels. The natural decline in gastric acid secretion that occurs with advancing age can make it difficult to absorb food bound B12 in meat, poultry, seafood, dairy, and eggs. For this reason, the Institute of Medicine recommends adults over the age of 50 get their B12 from fortified foods and/or supplements.

Prolonged use of PPI medication increases the risk of vitamin B12 deficiency. A review found taking PPI medications for more than two years doubled the odds of developing B12 deficiency, while another review found that metformin, a drug commonly used by those with type-2 diabetes, also causes a significant decline in B12. Around 40% of people with type-2 diabetes have acid reflux and many are placed on PPIs. This combination can be deadly as it increases the progression of diabetic neuropathy and causes declines in B12 and magnesium.

When you eat meat, poultry, fish, dairy or eggs, the acidic environment of your stomach separates the vitamin B12 from the protein to which it is attached. The parietal cells release intrinsic factor (IF) that binds the now freed B12 and transports it to the small intestine where it is absorbed. When you take an acid-suppressing medication, it makes that crucial process very difficult and over time, a deficiency can develop. Fortunately, B12 supplements and foods fortified with B12 do not require stomach acid for their absorption.

Deficiency Signs & Symptoms: No single sign has been uniquely associated with inadequate levels of vitamin B12. And by the time signs do show up, deficiency has often been present for some time. Symptoms can include paleness, fatigue, sore tongue, shortness of breath, heart palpitations, tingling in the hands and feet, weakness, depression, and personality changes. It's important to catch B12 deficiency early because some neurological effects are irreversible.

Which Kind: The B12 used in many dietary supplements is cyanocobalamin, a synthetic and inexpensive form. I recommend methylcobalamin, the natural form found in foods. Many people prefer sublingual drops, however, a head-to-head study found there was no difference in B12 levels between the group taking sublingual drops or in a tablet.

Dose: The recommended daily amount for adults is 2.4 mcg per day, though, older individuals often benefit from taking 20–40 mcg per day. You will need 1,000 mcg (1 mg) per day for 2–3 months to correct a B12 deficiency. I usually recommend 1,000 mcg per day for 8–12 weeks for anyone taking PPIs for longer than six months, especially if they are over the age of 50. If you are B12 deficient, follow the guidance from your health care professional.

Safety: There is no upper tolerable limit set for vitamin B12 as it is considered quite safe.

Vitamin C

Vitamin C, also called ascorbic acid, is involved in making collagen, converting tryptophan to serotonin, and is a cofactor in the synthesis of carnitine, thyroxin, norepinephrine, and dopamine. That means you need it for muscle strength, energy, wound healing, maintaining a healthy mood and immune response, and much more. But when it comes to getting enough vitamin C in our diet, Americans are falling short. In a large national survey using blood samples to determine the micronutrient status of Americans, researchers found that ~21 million Americans have serious vitamin C deficiency (levels consistent with scurvy), 66 million have marginal status, while fewer than 30 million have optimal vitamin C levels. Pretty shocking, given how critical vitamin C is for our immune defenses. Those 66 million people with marginal status could slip into a deficiency quickly if they get sick, as vitamin C levels decline rapidly during periods of illness and high stress.

Vitamin C is incredibly important for a healthy gut. In fact, the level of ascorbic acid in the gastric juices of your stomach are 3–8 times higher than the levels found in your blood. As a potent acid, it contributes to the overall acidity of our stomach, helping to protect us from harmful bacteria. It also protects the stomach from inflammation and damage by increasing prostaglandin E2 production by 90–100%, stimulating mucus (mucin) secretion to protect the stomach lining from acid, pepsin, alcohol, and NSAIDs. Vitamin C may also help prevent gastric cancer by acting as a potent antioxidant, preventing the formation of dietary nitrosamines, inhibiting infection by *H. pylori*, and improving treatment outcomes in people being treated for *H. pylori*.

But here is the problem: you must have stomach acid for vitamin C to be released into the gastric juices. Shut down stomach acid, you shut down ascorbic acid. In one study, it was found that at a gastric pH < 2, ascorbic acid levels in gastric juice were 16.5 µmol/L, but fell to 4.5 µmol/L when the gastric pH rose to 2–4, and *to zero* in those with a gastric pH > 6, not uncommon in those taking PPIs. Given the importance of vitamin C in the stomach, this is not good news. Shutting down stomach acid also lowers the vitamin C in your bloodstream. One study found that taking 40 mg of omeprazole per day caused mean plasma vitamin C levels to fall by 12.3% within just four weeks.

One of the best ways to get more vitamin C in your diet is to increase the amounts of fruits and vegetables you consume. Rich sources include citrus, peaches, peppers (sweet and chili), papayas, strawberries, and broccoli. Vitamin C is also plentiful in sardines and organ meats, though these are not exactly common in the American diet. Keep in mind, vitamin C levels in food drop during cooking and with prolonged storage.

Deficiency Signs & Symptoms: The most common signs of vitamin C deficiency are fatigue, bleeding gums, easy bruising, dry hair, and poorly healing wounds. Because vitamin C is needed to enhance the absorption of non-heme (plant-based) iron, iron deficiency anemia is common when vitamin C levels are low.

Which Kind: Taking a buffered vitamin C is best if you have heartburn. Some people prefer "natural" vitamin C. This is a legitimate preference, as the solvents used to make synthetic ascorbic acid are harsh, even if they are removed by the end of the process. However, both synthetic and natural ascorbic acid is used efficiently by the body; it really comes down to personal preference.

Dose: While the recommended daily intake is 90 mg per day for men and 75 mg for women, most experts believe the level should be closer to 400 mg per day. I agree. Many buffered vitamin C products contain 500–600 mg per serving, which is fine.

Safety: The upper limit for vitamin C has been set at 2,000 mg per day. Higher levels are not harmful, but diarrhea and GI upset can occur. The higher the single dose, the less vitamin C will be absorbed. Smaller, more frequent dosing is probably best.

Vitamins D and K

Vitamin D is involved in more than 1,000 biochemical actions in the body and plays a key role in maintaining optimal immune response, cardiovascular health, and regulating calcium and phosphorous levels, which are necessary for strong bones, muscle health, nerve conduction, and cellular function. Though there is little direct evidence that PPIs adversely affect vitamin D levels, it is important to ensure adequate levels, given the FDA mandated warning about these medications increasing the risk of fracture. Research shows that roughly 40% of Americans are deficient in vitamin D.

Vitamin K also plays an important role in regulating calcium. There are two primary forms of vitamin K—**K1**, found in in leafy green vegetables, with very small amounts present in dairy, and **K2**, found in fermented foods, such as natto, sauerkraut, cheese, egg yolks, ground beef, chicken liver and breast, and butter from grass-fed cows. Much of K1 is converted to K2 by gut bacteria. K2 directs calcium towards our bones and teeth and away from tissues where it doesn't belong, such as our blood vessels and breasts. Vitamin K2 also activates matrix Gla-protein (MGP), a potent inhibitor of arterial and soft tissue calcification.

We need calcium in our diet, vitamin D to absorb dietary calcium, magnesium to convert vitamin D to its most active form, and vitamin K (particularly K2) to direct the calcium to our bones. If you want healthy bones, in addition to regular weight bearing exercise, you need to ensure you have adequate amounts of these important nutrients.

Deficiency Signs and Symptoms: For most people, mild vitamin D deficiency does not produce any overt signs. More severe vitamin D deficiency in infancy or childhood leads to rickets, with bowed legs and rib cage deformities, and seizures caused by low levels of blood calcium. In adults, osteomalacia develops, characterized by weak and painful muscles and bones.

Vitamin K deficiency can cause bleeding gums, easy bruising, and heavy menstrual periods. It can also lead to brittle bones and calcifications in blood vessels and soft tissues in the body.

Which Kind: All formal recommendations for vitamin D are for cholecalciferol, or vitamin D3. Ergocalciferol, or vitamin D2, is found in plants and may be preferred by vegans. Vitamin D3 does have an edge when it comes to raising serum vitamin D levels, however, either will get the job done if taken in sufficient quantity. Vitamin K comes as either K1, K2 or a combination of the two, which is what I generally recommend.

Dose: The recommended daily intake for vitamin D3 is 600 IU per day until age 70, increasing to 800 IU per day for those 71 years and older. In my own experience, I find this intake level insufficient to maintain adequate vitamin D levels year-round. I generally recommend 2,000 IU vitamin D3 per day. The best way to know how much vitamin D you *really need* is to have your levels checked with a simple 25(OH)D blood test. Ask your health care professional to check your vitamin D level or order your own test. If you are deficient in vitamin D, it takes *much higher doses* to correct the deficiency, generally 50,000 IU per week for 8–12 weeks. The Endocrine Society set the lower normal limit for serum 25(OH)D at 30 ng/mL. Anything under 20 ng/mL is considered vitamin D deficiency. Many experts feel that for immune and bone health, the 25(OH)D level should be closer to 40 ng/mL (100 nmol/L). For most patients, I aim for 40–50 ng/mL.

The recommended daily intake for vitamin K is 120 mcg per day for men and 90 mcg per day for women. The recommended daily intake only pertains to vitamin K1, there is no level set for K2. In general, I recommend taking a mixture of K1 and K2 of 90–120 mcg per day.

Safety: For vitamin D, the tolerable upper limit has been set at 4,000 IU per day for those 9 years of age and older. This means that the vast majority of people can take this level without causing themselves harm. To learn more about vitamin D, click here.

There is no tolerable upper limit set for vitamin K. There have been no reports of toxicity associated with high intakes of vitamin K.

If you are taking warfarin (Coumadin) you should not take *supplemental* vitamin K without talking to your health care professional first.

CHAPTER 10

Protocol for Healing Heartburn Naturally

> *If you are currently taking a PPI, please proceed to Chapter 11 and follow the PPI Tapering Protocol. The following protocol is for those who have reflux but are not taking daily PPI medications.*

Now that you have learned about the importance of a properly functioning digestive system, I want to share my eight–week protocol to help you get rid of your heartburn, improve LES function, heal irritated tissues, and restore your gut microbiome. I have used this approach for hundreds of patients over the years and feel confident that if you follow these recommendations faithfully, you can get your heartburn under control.

Weeks 1–8

Low Glycemic Diet: One of the most important things you can do to get rid of heartburn, bloating, and indigestion is to slash the refined carbs in your diet. I know changing your diet can be incredibly challenging. And I also know that it is one of the most powerful levers you can pull when it comes to getting your GI tract in order. Plus, you will have more energy, less hunger, feel lighter, improve your metabolism and digestion, and eradicate your heartburn.

For the next eight weeks, you need to follow a low glycemic load/low-carb diet. Some of my patients have preferred a ketogenic approach, though it takes more commitment. The main thing both of these dietary approaches have in common—and the part that is most important for eliminating reflux—is a *dramatic reduction* in refined grains (e.g., white bread, cereals, cookies, donuts, white rice), sweetened beverages (e.g., soda, juice), white potatoes, and foods with added sugars. **Instead, there is an emphasis on healthy proteins, healthy fats, fresh veggies and fresh fruits.** Greek yogurt and berries, or veggie omelet for breakfast. A loaded salad for lunch with spinach, grilled chicken and/or beans, grapes, and olive oil/vinegar dressing. Grilled salmon or chicken breast with baked sweet potato or steamed broccoli for dinner.

There are books and apps that can be helpful in getting you successfully launched on your new diet plan. You will need help on this journey, but I can promise it is worth the effort. See the Resources section for recommendations.

Do not eat *anything* three hours before bed. Be disciplined and plan ahead. If you go to bed at 10 PM, then nothing after 7 PM. If you find yourself finishing dinner at 8 PM, then try to stay upright until 11 PM. Late night eating is one of the quickest ways to sabotage your entire plan.

No carbonated beverages or alcohol and avoid any of your known dietary **triggers.**

If possible, go for **a 20-minute walk** after dinner. Grab your partner, your kids, or your dog and go for a stroll. Or just put on your headphones and listen to music or a podcast.

Sleep on your left side and/or elevate the head of your bed with blocks or wedge pillow.

Add **Melatonin:** Start taking 5–6 mg of fast acting melatonin 60–90 minutes before your scheduled bedtime. Melatonin helps strengthen the tone of the LES. Studies show that taking just 5–6 mg of melatonin at night works as well as PPIs by eight weeks.

Add **Digestive Enzymes:** Many people I see with reflux have poor digestive function. In addition to heartburn, they also have gas and bloating after a meal. I generally advise taking a broad-spectrum digestive enzyme for eight weeks, as you work to get your heartburn under control. Look for a product with enzymes that digest protein (e.g., protease, papain and/or bromelain), carbohydrates (e.g., amylase, cellulase, and/or lactase), fats (e.g., lipase), and possibly beans (e.g., alpha-galactosidase). See Resources section for examples. Take as directed *before* the main meals of the day. Keep them on your kitchen table to make it easier to remember to take them. And make sure you keep some in your bag for meals on the go. *Talk to your health care professional* **prior** *to taking enzymes that digest protein if you have a history of stomach ulcers.*

Add **Botanicals:** During the weaning process, botanicals can help prevent rebound hyperacidity, support LES function, reduce reflux episodes, and soothe irritated tissue. Aloe vera gel is foundational and should be taken twice daily. Alginate acts a physical barrier to prevent reflux when taken after meals. Artichoke leaf and/or amla improve gastric motility. Marshmallow root, DGL, or slippery elm are all excellent for breakthrough reflux, working quickly to soothe irritated tissue. There are numerous products on the market that contain these ingredients. Refer to Chapter 6 for detailed information about dosing and use. See Resources section for examples of products.

Add **Probiotics:** Take specific probiotic strains to help reduce GERD symptoms, as well as colonize the stomach and intestines. Look for products that contain one or more of the following strains: *Lactobacillus reuteri* DSM 17938, *Lactobacillus plantarum* 299v, *Lactobacillus reuteri, Lactobacillus gasseiri, Lactobacillus paracasei* F19, or *Bacillus subtilis.* See Resource section for more direction.

Weeks 8–12

Congratulations! You have now completed eight weeks towards better gut health! It is critically important not to go back to eating too many refined carbs or eating late at night. Don't undo all the great progress you have made! However, it is time to **see if you can wean off some of your supplements.** I recommend doing this one week and one supplement at a time. *If your symptoms return, restart that* *supplement and take for another four weeks.* Then try going off of it again. All of these supplements have excellent long-term safety profiles if you need to continue taking them. I just believe in not taking supplements longer than necessary.

- **Discontinue your digestive enzymes during week 9.** See if you notice any bloating, gassiness or reflux. If symptoms return, start taking them again for four weeks, and then try discontinuing them again.
- **During week 10, discontinue melatonin.** Again, look for any changes in reflux and digestion. If symptoms return, restart your melatonin for another four weeks, and then try discontinuing it again.
- **During week 11, discontinue probiotics.** Look for any changes in reflux, bloating or stooling. If symptoms return, restart probiotics for another four weeks, and then try discontinuing them again.
- **Use your botanicals as needed for occasional heartburn.**

CHAPTER 11

Protocol for Tapering off PPI Medication

> *If you want to wean off your PPI medication, please talk to your health care provider first to make sure it is appropriate.*

I am going to share a 12-week PPI tapering protocol that I have used in my practice with excellent success. Weaning off your PPIs is extremely important if you've been taking them longer than 3–4 months. With higher gastric pH, the hormone gastrin becomes elevated. If you stop taking your PPI suddenly, it can cause a huge spike in acid production. Slowly tapering allows you to incorporate dietary and supplement regimens into your daily life, while reducing your PPI dose *and* avoiding rebound hyperacidity. **During this taper, you will wean off your PPI—or get to the lowest possible dose that keeps your reflux under control—heal irritated tissues, improve**

LES function, restore healthy gut microbiota, and replenish crucial micronutrients. The protocol is divided into three parts:

Remove: The first two weeks are dedicated to removing reflux triggers and implementing important lifestyle changes. You are setting the stage for success.

Replace: During the subsequent six weeks you will gradually replace your PPIs with safe and effective natural remedies.

Restore: The final four weeks are designed to ensure you have restored optimal digestive function and replenished any micronutrient shortcomings.

Weeks 1–2

These first two weeks are all about preparation. You will stay on your current PPI medication as you work to remove some of the biggest triggers for reflux: refined carbohydrates, carbonated and sugary beverages, late night eating, and poor sleep position!

Low Glycemic Diet: One of the most impactful changes you can make to get rid of heartburn, bloating, and indigestion is to slash the refined carbs in your diet. I know changing your diet can be incredibly challenging. I also know it is one of the most powerful levers you can pull when it comes to getting your GI tract in order. *Plus, you will have more energy, less hunger, feel lighter, improve your metabolism and digestion, and eradicate your heartburn.*

For the next 12 weeks, you need to follow a low glycemic load/low-carb diet. Some of my patients have preferred a ketogenic approach, though it takes more commitment. The main thing both of these dietary approaches have in common—and the part that is most important for eliminating reflux—is a *dramatic reduction* in refined grains (e.g., white bread, cereals, cookies, donuts, white rice), sweetened beverages (e.g., soda, juice), white potatoes, and foods with added sugars. **Instead, there is an emphasis on healthy proteins, healthy fats, fresh veggies and fresh fruits.** Try Greek yogurt and berries, or veggie omelet for breakfast. A loaded salad for lunch with spinach, grilled chicken and/or beans, grapes, and olive oil/vinegar dressing. Grilled salmon or chicken breast with baked sweet potato or steamed broccoli for dinner.

There are books and apps that can be helpful in getting you successfully launched on your new diet plan. I promise it will be worth the effort. See the Resources section for recommendations.

Do not eat *anything* three hours before bed. Be disciplined and plan ahead. If you go to bed at 10 PM, then nothing after 7 PM. If you find yourself finishing dinner at 8 PM, then try to stay upright until 11 PM. Late night eating is one of the quickest ways to sabotage your entire plan.

No carbonated beverages or alcohol and avoid any of your known dietary **triggers.**

If possible, go for **a 20-minute walk** after dinner. Grab your partner, your kids, or your dog and go for a stroll. Or just put on your headphones and listen to music or a podcast.

Sleep on your left side and/or elevate the head of your bed with blocks or wedge pillow.

Add **Melatonin:** Start taking 5–6 mg of fast acting melatonin 60–90 minutes before your scheduled bedtime. Melatonin helps strengthen the tone of the LES. Studies show that taking just 5–6 mg of melatonin at night works as well as PPIs by eight weeks.

Weeks 2–8

Now that your low carb diet is well underway, **you'll begin weaning you off your PPI medication and replacing it with botanicals and supplements** that will ensure proper gastric motility, enhance the tone of the LES, nourish the gut microbiome, and soothe and protect the esophagus, stomach, and small intestine. Continue taking your melatonin and add the following supplements. *(For resources and product suggestions, please refer to the Resources section).*

Add **Digestive enzymes:** As you wean off your PPI, you'll provide digestive support by adding a broad-spectrum digestive enzyme. Look for a product with enzymes that digest protein (e.g., protease, papain and/or bromelain), carbohydrates (e.g., amylase, cellulase, and/or lactase), fats (e.g., lipase), and possibly beans (e.g., alpha-galactosidase). For recommendations, review the Resources section. Take as directed *before* the main meals of the day. Keep them on your kitchen table to make it easier to remember to take them. And make sure you keep some in your bag for meals on the go. *Talk to your health care professional **prior** to taking enzymes that digest protein if you have a history of stomach ulcers.*

Add **Botanicals:** During the weaning process, botanicals can help prevent rebound hyperacidity, support LES function, reduce reflux episodes, and soothe irritated tissue. Aloe vera gel is foundational and should be taken twice daily. Alginate acts a physical barrier to prevent reflux when taken after meals. Artichoke leaf and/or amla improve gastric motility. Marshmallow root, DGL, or slippery elm, are all excellent for breakthrough reflux, working quickly to soothe irritated tissue. There are numerous products on the market that contain these ingredients. Refer to Chapter 6 for detailed information about dosing and use, and the Resources section for recommendations.

Add **Probiotics:** Take specific probiotic strains to help reduce GERD symptoms, as well as colonize the stomach and intestines. Look for products that contain one or more of the following strains: *Lactobacillus reuteri* DSM 17938, *Lactobacillus plantarum* 299v, *Lactobacillus reuteri, Lactobacillus gasseiri, Lactobacillus paracasei* F19, or *Bacillus subtilis.* Review the Resources section for recommendations.

Add **Magnesium:** PPIs can dramatically lower magnesium levels, which can be dangerous to your overall health. Magnesium is best taken in the evening, as it relaxes muscles, helps prepare you for sleep, and can help stave off nighttime reflux. Take 400 mg magnesium each night before going to bed. Look for a product that contains magnesium *malate,* citrate, and/or glycinate. Decrease your dose if stools are loose.

Add a Multivitamin and Vitamin B12: PPIs can reduce vitamin B12 levels. Take 1,000 mcg (1 mg) methylcobalamin once per day, with or without food. I also recommend taking an age and gender-based multivitamin to shore up against any gaps that may have occurred as the result of diet and/or acid suppression.

Weeks 2–4

Decrease PPI: Decrease your PPI dose by 50%. For instance, if you are taking 40 mg of esomeprazole per day, reduce it to 20 mg. Switching to omeprazole can be useful for titrating your dose if your current PPI has limited dosing options. As you wean off your PPI, if you have three or more reflux episodes over the course of a week, increase your botanicals. If needed, add an H2 blocker. I generally recommend 20 mg of famotidine (Pepcid) either before dinner or bedtime. Talk to your local pharmacist or health care provider if you have questions about which H2 blocker is best for you. If this does not control your reflux, take your PPI dose back up for a week and then try to reduce the dose again.

Weeks 4–6

Decrease PPI: If you are having two or less reflux episodes per week, then decrease your PPI dose again by 50%. If you are having three or more reflux episodes per week, stay at your current dose, continue taking your H2 blocker, and increase the frequency/dose of alginate and aloe vera gel. If this does not control your reflux, take your PPI dose back up for a week and then try to decrease the dose again.

Weeks 6–8

Decrease PPI: If you are having two or fewer reflux episodes per week, discontinue your PPI. While not common, if you are still having three or more reflux episodes per week with your PPI, H2 blocker and botanicals, go back to the last PPI dose that was controlling your symptoms and proceed to Chapter 12.

Weeks 8–12

At this point, you should be off or almost off your PPI medication. It can be tempting to go back to old habits but don't undo all the great progress you have made. It is so crucial to keep highly refined carbs in check and avoid late night eating. **Pay attention to triggers**. If you want to have a glass of wine with dinner, have just one glass and note if you have reflux. Go slow. Over these next four weeks, you will taper you off your supplements one at a time, one week at a time. If your symptoms return, restart that supplement, and take for another four weeks, then try going off it again. All of these supplements have excellent long-term safety profiles if you need to continue taking them.

- During week 9, discontinue your vitamin B12. Continue your multivitamin that includes a range of Bs, including B12, and your magnesium.
- During week 10, discontinue digestive enzymes. If you notice a change in bloating, gassiness, or reflux—restart your enzymes.
- During week 11, discontinue melatonin. If you notice any changes in reflux or digestion—restart your melatonin.
- During week 12, discontinue probiotics. If you notice any changes in reflux, bloating, or stooling—restart your probiotics.

End of Week 12

Congratulations! You have now completed your 12 weeks towards better gut health! **It is vitally important that you continue these dietary and lifestyle recommendations to prevent your reflux from returning.** *Pay attention to triggers.* Continue to take your multivitamin and magnesium and use your botanicals and/or H2 blocker as needed for occasional heartburn.

CHAPTER 12

Protocol for Those Taking PPI Medication Long-Term

If your healthcare provider has recommended that you stay on your PPI medication for an extended period, perhaps indefinitely, there are dietary and lifestyle strategies that can keep you feeling your best. Make sure that you are own best advocate when it comes to your health. Discuss any concerns you may have about taking PPIs long-term and request certain laboratory tests to monitor kidney function and key micronutrients. The following tests, in my opinion, should be performed and monitored annually in someone taking PPIs long-term:

- *Serum B12 and/or methylmalonic acid* (a more sensitive indicator of B12 status).

- *Serum magnesium* is usually ordered to evaluate magnesium status, but a normal level (1.7–2.3 mg/dL for adults) doesn't mean you don't have a deficiency, as magnesium is primarily intracellular. If this test comes back low—you are *definitely* magnesium deficient. Monitoring red blood cell magnesium level *may* be a better indicator.
- *Serum 25(OH)D* to check your vitamin D level in order to optimize bone health. A range of 30–50 ng/mL is considered "normal."
- *Serum ferritin* is the one of best tests to determine if iron levels are normal. If it is low further tests may be ordered but a cutoff of ≤ 30 ng/mL is highly specific for iron deficiency anemia.
- *Serum creatinine/GFR* tests to evaluate the function of your kidneys.

While monitoring for deficiencies is important, prevention is absolutely "worth a pound of cure." By understanding the role of stomach acid in digestion, we can predict where problems may arise over time. Sensible steps can be taken to reduce potential risk.

In previous chapters I have outlined how diet, sleep and sleep position, and other lifestyle strategies can reduce the frequency and severity of GERD. Many of these recommendations hold true even if you are taking PPIs long-term, especially if you occasionally have breakthrough reflux. However, there are some specific supplements that I recommend when it comes to chronic PPI use. I have provided resources and recommendations that might further guide you in the Resources section of this book.

Digestive enzymes: PPIs shut down stomach acid, thereby preventing the release of HCl and the activation of the key enzyme in protein digestion, pepsin. Taking a product with enzymes that digest protein (e.g., protease, papain and/or bromelain) is *very important.* Many products also include enzymes for digesting carbohydrates (e.g., amylase, cellulase, and/or lactase), fats (e.g., lipase), and possibly beans (e.g., alpha-galactosidase). In general, using a broad-spectrum digestive enzyme works best. Take as directed *before* the main meals of the day. Keep them on your kitchen table to make it easier to remember to take them. And make sure you keep some in your bag for meals on the go. *Talk to your health care professional **prior** to taking enzymes that digest protein if you have a history of stomach ulcers.*

I often recommend betaine HCl with the main protein-rich meal of the day for my patients on long-term PPIs, *who DO NOT have a history of stomach ulcers.* I discussed the rationale for this in Chapter 7. *Only use higher doses of betaine HCl in partnership with a knowledgeable health care provider.* Most functional, integrative, and naturopathic physicians and practitioners are trained in how to safely titrate betaine HCl.

Probiotics: Take specific probiotic strains to support your microbiota. It is crucial that you do what you can to reduce your risk of *C. difficile* and other gastrointestinal infections. Go to usprobioticguide.com and search under adult health for probiotic products that have been clinically shown to reduce the risk for *C. difficile* and other community acquired infections. Take as directed.

Magnesium: PPIs can dramatically lower magnesium levels, which can be dangerous to your overall health. Magnesium is best taken in the evening, as it relaxes muscles, helps prepare you for sleep, and can help stave off nighttime reflux. Take 400 mg of magnesium each night before going to bed. Look for a product that contains magnesium *malate,* citrate, and/or glycinate. Decrease your dose if you experience diarrhea. *Note:* your practitioner might recommend higher doses based upon clinical judgment and lab tests. But this is a safe and effective dose for most.

Multivitamin and Vitamin B12: PPIs can reduce vitamin B12 levels. *Supplemental forms of B12 do not require gastric acid for absorption.* Make sure you are taking 250–500 mcg per day of methylcobalamin. I also recommend taking an age and gender-based multivitamin to shore up against any gaps that may occur as the result of diet and/or acid suppression.

Vitamin C: PPIs can lower vitamin C levels. Increase your intake of fresh fruits and vegetables and take 200–400 mg of buffered vitamin C per day with a meal.

APPENDIX 1

Clinician Directed **Protocol of Betaine HCl**

The following protocol is used by many integrative and functional medicine practitioners to determine if an individual's symptoms are due *to low stomach acid:*

- Have patient take one capsule/tablet of betaine HCl (500–700 mg) immediately before eating a protein containing meal. Have them watch for any feelings of discomfort (e.g., heartburn, stomach pain, back pain). If they feel any burning or pain, instruct them to mix 1 tsp. of baking soda in a glass of water and drink it to neutralize the acid. If the patient experiences discomfort with one capsule/tablet, discontinue the trial altogether.
- After two days, if the patient hasn't experienced any discomfort, increase to two capsules/tablets immediately before eating a protein-containing meal. Again, instruct them

to watch for any feelings of discomfort. If they feel any burning or pain, neutralize the acid with baking soda and then bring them back down to 1 tablet/capsule before the main protein containing meal of the day.

- After two days at this dose, if they still haven't felt any discomfort, increase to three capsules/tablets immediately before eating a protein-containing meal. Again, have them watch for any feelings of discomfort. If they experience any discomfort, have them neutralize the acid with baking soda and back the dose down to 2 capsules/tablets.

- In my experience, most people experience discomfort at a dose of 2,000–3,000 mg. Do not exceed 3,000 mg. It is absolutely critical to instruct the patient to only take betaine HCl when they eat a protein-rich meal. Dosing should be reduced, or the product NOT taken, if it is a smaller meal.

Important Notes:

- The supplement is betaine HCl. Betaine is a compound naturally found in beets, spinach, wheat bran and other foods and is safe.

- Do not confuse betaine HCl with betaine trimethylglycine (TMG). These are two very different compounds and are used for different purposes.

- Betaine HCl must be taken in a tablet or capsule to avoid the HCl from coming into contact with the esophagus. Do not open a capsule and pour onto food or in liquid.

- Betaine HCl is contraindicated in those with peptic ulcer disease (now or in the past).

- Remember to instruct the patient to never take this supplement on an empty stomach unless followed immediately by a protein-containing meal.

APPENDIX 2

Resources

People often ask me about books, brands, and other resources so I have included a few of my favorite here. This is by no means an exhaustive list. Your health care professional may recommend a different brand, product, or resource. Please note, products may be discontinued, serving size of supplements may change, links may no longer be active. Be a savvy and educated consumer.

DIET RESOURCES

- BOOK: *Savor* by Thich Nhat Hanh—one of my most favorite books on mindful eating.
- BOOK: *Simply Keto* by Suzanne Ryan—very good book for beginners who are interested in the ketogenic diet.
- BOOK: *The Glycemic Load Diet* by Rob Thompson— excellent book for learning how to follow a low-glycemic load diet. Super practical.

- BOOK: *The Low Glycal Diet* by Jeffrey Dunham —an awesome blend of low glycemic load and low carb dietary strategies.
- APP: *Low-Glycal Diet*™ —partners with the book above. Great way to keep track of your glycemic load, as well as calories. Works better on iPhone than Android, though.
- APP: *Carb Manager* —probably my favorite app for keeping track of carbs. Available for iPhone and Android.
- APP: *Senza: Keto & Fasting*—one of the best apps for keto diet, while also integrating fasting if you choose.

SLEEP AND STRESS RESOURCES

- APP: The American Sleep Association has put together a list of the highest rated apps for sleep.
- APP: *CBT-I Coach* is a program developed by the Veteran's Administration, Stanford School of Medicine and the Dept of Defense's National Center for Telehealth and Technology. Using cognitive behavioral techniques, it is designed to help those with chronic sleep problems.
- APP: VeryWell Mind has put together a nice list of apps that can help you manage your stress.
- **Now Foods Melatonin** 5 mg: Good quality brand at a good price. Melatonin capsules. Typical use: one capsule 60–90 minutes before bed.
- **MegaFood Melatonin Berry Good Sleep** 3 mg: Nice chewable gummy in a base of berries, with no flavorings, gelatin, high fructose corn syrup, and less than 2 grams of sugar per serving. Typical use: two in the evening 60–90 minutes before bed.

PROBIOTIC RESOURCE

- WEBSITE: *Clinical Guide to Probiotic Products Available in USA*—a great site for finding probiotic products that contain clinically tested strains at the correct dose for specific health issues. The evidence is ranked from 1–3 with level 1 being the highest. You want to consider those products with level 1 evidence for CDAD prevention (*C. difficile* associated diarrhea), HP (*Helicobacter pylori*) adjunct to standard eradication therapy, and CID (Common infectious disease) community acquired. Here are some examples:

Bio-K+Biome PRO and *Bio-K+Biome*: level 1 evidence for CDAD

BioGaia Protectis: level 1 evidence for HP

Culturelle Products: level 1 evidence for HP

DanActiv Actimel: level 1 evidence for CID

Florastor and Florastor Max: level 1 evidence for CDAD and HP

UltraFlora Immune Booster: level 1 evidence for CID

Yakult: level 1 evidence for CID

DIGESTIVE ENZYMES

There are many digestive enzyme products on the market, many with lots of "extras" such as probiotics and herbs. Most of the time the probiotics are not the strains you need, and the herbs are too low a potency to be beneficial. The products below contain only plant or microbial derived enzymes and are of high quality. Take as directed.

- ***Metagenics SpectraZyme Complete***: Very high-quality brand. This product contains non-animal derived enzymes for the digestion of proteins (proteases stable across pH), carbohydrates, fats, cellulose, and lactose.

- **Pure Encapsulations Digestive Enzymes Ultra:** Very high-quality brand. This vegetarian based product includes enzymes for the digestion of proteins, fats, carbohydrates, dairy, beans, and fiber.
- **Thorne Research Plantizyme:** Very-high quality brand. Contains plant-based enzymes for digestion of protein, carbs, fats and fiber.

MAGNESIUM

MegaFood Relax & Calm Magnesium Powder: I formulated these products with MegaFood, a very high-quality brand. The powder provides 300 mg per serving of magnesium citrate, malate, and glycinate. Available in two flavors. There are also magnesium chews that contain 250 mg of magnesium malate and citrate.

Now Foods Magnesium Citrate: A good company with reasonably priced supplements. Contains a blend of magnesium citrate, malate, and glycinate. Three soft gels deliver 400 mg. *Note: this is not a vegetarian product as it contains bovine gelatin.*

VITAMIN B12

Blue Bonnet Methylcobalamin Earth Sweet Chewables 1,000 mcg: A clean chewable B12.

Pure Encapsulations Methylcobalamin 1,000 mcg: Available in capsules and liquid.

Thorne Research Methylcobalamin 1,000 mcg: Available in capsules

VITAMIN C

Vital Nutrients Buffered C for Sensitive Individuals 500 mg: Very good brand. Buffered vitamin C is designed for GI comfort. Typical use: one capsule per day.

Now Foods Calcium Ascorbate Buffered C 500 mg: Buffered with calcium ascorbate. Easy on the stomach. Typical use: one capsule per day.

BOTANICALS

Rightful Digestive Relief and Repair: I formulated this product in a soothing liquid base of aloe vera gel (22,800 mg from inner fillet), with alginate (500 mg), DGL (350 mg extract equivalent to 1.4 grams licorice, <1% glycyrrhizin), artichoke leaf (300 mg extract), chamomile flower (250 mg extract equivalent to 1,000 mg chamomile), marshmallow root (250 mg extract equivalent to 1,000 mg marshmallow), amla (250 mg Indian gooseberry fruit), mastic gum (100 mg), and potassium bicarbonate (40 mg). Typical use: take one ounce before or immediately after meals and at bedtime, as needed.

Lily of the Desert Organic Aloe Vera Juice, Inner Fillet: Very high-quality aloe vera juice (less than 1 ppm of aloin). Typical use: 1–2 ounces before or after meals and at bedtime, as needed.

Nature's Way DGL Chewable Tablets 75 mg: A reputable high-quality brand. Instructions on label are to take three tablets in the morning and three at night. It contains no fructose.

Solaray Artichoke Leaf Extract: Reputable brand. This is a standardized extract delivering 300 mg per capsule. Typical use: take one capsule 1–2 times per day.

Traditional Medicinals Teas: Very high-quality medicinal-tea company. There are three that I want to point out. *Organic Chamomile* tea if you just want something to help you relax and soothe your stomach. *Organic Ginger with Chamomile* tea will give you the added digestive benefit of ginger along with chamomile. And *Organic Throat Coat* (original with slippery elm) is generally recommended for colds and coughs, however the licorice, marshmallow, and slippery elm make it a great tea to keep around to soothe occasional heartburn.

Mastiqe Sugar Free Chewing Gum: Mastic chewing gum. Great to chew a couple times per day for oral hygiene, fresh breath, and to ease occasional heartburn. Comes in plain, spearmint, and peppermint. I would choose the plain or spearmint (avoid peppermint when dealing with heartburn).

Banyan Botanicals Amalaki (amla): Very reliable company for Indian or Ayurvedic herbs. Each tablet provides 500 mg of amla fruit. They recommend 1 to 2 tablets per day.